THE BLACK AND TANS

THE BLACK
AND TANS

by
Richard Bennett

SPELLMOUNT
Staplehurst

British Library Cataloguing in Publication Data:
A catalogue record for this book is available
from the British Library

Copyright © Richard Bennett 1959, 2001

ISBN 1-86227-098-8

This edition published in the UK in 2001 by
Spellmount Limited
The Old Rectory
Staplehurst
Kent TN12 0AZ
United Kingdom

Tel: 01580 893730
Fax: 01580 893731
E-mail: enquiries@spellmount.com
Website: www.spellmount.com

3 5 7 9 8 6 4 2

The right of Richard Bennett to be identified
as the author of this work has been asserted by him
in accordance with the Copyright, Designs
and Patents Act 1988

Printed in Great Britain by
TJ International Ltd, Padstow, Cornwall

CONTENTS

LIST OF ILLUSTRATIONS

LIST OF ILLUSTRATIONS

ACKNOWLEDGEMENTS

The extracts from Sir Henry Wilson's diaries have been taken, with the permission of the owner of the copyright, from Major-General C. E. Calwell's *Sir Henry Wilson: His Life and Diaries*, published by Cassell's; and those from General Macready's *Annals of an Active Life* by permission of the publishers, Hutchinson. I am greatly indebted to Mr. Paddy Malley who allowed me to study his brother Ernie O'Malley's papers, and to Mr. Cathal O'Shannon who gave me invaluable advice about sources and also lent me contemporary material. Neither can be held responsible for my opinions. Nor can the many participants on both sides who have kindly spared me their time and given me the benefit of their advice. I have been unable to trace the writer of the manuscript quoted on pages 161–3 and must make an anonymous acknowledgement to the author who is, I hope, still with us. I would also like to thank Mr. S. G. Pryor of the *News Chronicle* Library for the help he gave me with my researches.

Grateful Acknowledgements for the illustrations should be made as follows:

Mr. J. Cashman, Dublin, 1, 2, 3, 4, 5, 6, 7, 11, 12, 14, 15, 17, 18, 20, 22, 23, 24, 25, 26, 27, 28, 34, 40, 47, 48.

Central News, 29.

Central Press, 36.

The Cork *Examiner*, 38, 39.

Mr. Paddy Malley, 32, 35.

National Museum of Ireland, 21, 30.

Radio Times Hulton Picture Library, 8, 9, 10, 16, 19, 31, 33, 41, 42, 43, 44, 45, 46.

CHAPTER ONE

The Beginning of the End

ON NEW YEAR'S DAY, 1919, an English sentry surveyed the Irish scene, no doubt with soldierly indifference, from the top of the old Castle keep in Dublin. He could follow the line of the Liffey below him on its way to the sea, and look over the roofs of the city to the damp green fields climbing into the Dublin hills. For six hundred years his military predecessors had stood at this point, armed with crossbow, hackbut and musket, scrutinising this dismal prospect. Today machine guns were mounted behind the parapet under the fluttering Union Jack. An infantry guard in steel helmets was stationed in the courtyard below, where two armoured cars and a tank were manned and ready for action and two Sappers were down a manhole, testing the wire entanglements across the subterranean River Poddle.

There was trouble in the land, as so often before. On the 28th December, 1918, the post-war General Election results had brought an overwhelming victory in Ireland for the Sinn Fein party, which won seventy-three out of a hundred and five seats. Sinn Fein had declared that it would not send its elected representatives to Westminster to join the members who had been returned 'to hang the Kaiser'. It had resolved, instead, to sever Ireland's connection with the United Kingdom and to set up its own independent Republican Government. Commenting on the results, Mr. Shortt, the Secretary for Ireland, said on New Year's Eve that the Irish question would be settled 'Peaceably or bloodily within the next six months'.

[9]

He was wrong. Nor was there any doubt of the way in which the issue would be settled. On the 17th January, 1919 Sir Henry Wilson, Chief of the Imperial General Staff, noted in his diary: 'We are sitting on top of a mine which may go up at any minute. Ireland tonight has telegraphed for some more tanks and machine guns, and are evidently anxious about the state of the country'! The Dáil Eireann met four days later to declare its independence and to pledge itself and the Irish people 'to make this declaration effective by every means at our command'. De Valera, the President, and Arthur Griffith, the founder of Sinn Fein, were two of the thirty-six elected members who were in gaol. Had they been at liberty, they might have avoided this intransigent declaration of a Republic which allowed no possibility of manœuvre or retreat and could only lead to more unnecessary bloodshed. On the same day, the 21st January, Dan Breen, Séan Treacy and several other Irish Volunteers ambushed and killed two policemen of the Royal Irish Constabulary who were escorting a cart with a load of gelignite for Soloheadbeg quarry. The ambushers had fired the first shots in a guerilla war against the Crown Forces.

How had Anglo-Irish relations come to this sad impasse? There are Irishmen who trace the story back to 1172, the days of Strongbow, and the outlawing of the Irish by the Normans. Others, with less retentive historical memories, start at the dispossession of the natives and the planting of colonists under the Tudors and Stuarts. Many are content to remember Cromwell's massacres at Drogheda and Wexford as the beginning of English iniquity. Nearly all know of the penal laws of the seventeenth century, the rebellions of 1798 and 1803, the depopulation of the island, and its economic spoliation after the union of the Parliaments of Great Britain and Ireland in 1800, when the cross of St. Patrick joined the crosses of St. George and St. Andrew to make the flag which came to be known as the

Union Jack. Every Englishman was horrified by the famine of 1846–47, and many spoke against the colonial rule by Coercion Acts and Crime Acts in the nineteenth century. But they were never numerous or powerful enough, either inside or outside the House of Commons, to help steer Irish Home Rule through the cross currents of party politics at Westminster. The catalogue of Irish distress is long and no credit to England. 'Anglo-Irish history,' it has been said, 'is for Englishmen to remember, for Irishmen to forget'!

But at the turn of the century Ireland was peaceful, if not free. It was agreed that the country had never been so quiet for six hundred years. The penal laws were a memory, though an abiding one, and the Land Purchase Act had once more given Irish tenants a stake in their own country. The Irish Republican Brotherhood, a secret society, which had been founded in 1858 to establish an Irish Republic by force, was only a handful of zealots who could make no headway, although they were later to leaven the lump. Ireland, greatly over-represented with the one hundred and five members and the majority for Home Rule, had weight to throw about in Westminster, and it seemed that Home Rule could not long be delayed.

As so often, the movement for revolt came not when things were at their worst but when they were getting better. The Gaelic League, founded in 1893, had inspired a renaissance of Irish culture, awakened a civilised nationalist pride and prepared the ground for Arthur Griffith who founded Sinn Fein in 1905. The words mean 'Ourselves', or 'We are it', and have denoted both a sturdy independence and a narrow parochialism. The aim of the movement was to reduce the British Administration by passive resistance, and to establish an Irish Government in its place. Griffith, who proposed a 'dual crown' and not a republic, claimed to have borrowed his ideas from the Hungarian patriot, Déak. He was an able journalist and a man of moderate views.

At the same time, the Socialist, James Connolly, was organising Irish labour, both industrially and politically, with the openly declared aim of establishing an Irish Socialist Republic. He also drew his inspiration from sources outside Ireland. 'Only the Irish working class remains as the incorruptible inheritors of the fight for freedom in Ireland,' he wrote. Such words, which enlarged the vocabulary of independence to the dismay of prosperous Sinn Feiners, were to win Socialist allies for Irish independence across the seas.

Something had to be done about Ireland. No one disputed it. Asquith's Liberal Government accordingly passed an Irish Home Rule Bill in 1912, for which no Irish member voted. It conferred only limited powers on a Dublin Parliament, but even so the Lords rejected it decisively, and the Bill could not, therefore, become law until 1914. By that time Sir Edward Carson had organised armed resistance to the British Government's proposals in Protestant Ulster. This Irishman was, perhaps, best known to the public as the formidable advocate, who counted among his successes the conviction of his compatriot, Oscar Wilde. Armed Ulster Volunteers drilled openly, prepared to face death rather than submit to any form of government from Dublin. In April a cargo of German arms was run into Northern Irish ports. The South naturally retaliated by forming the National Volunteers. In July, Erskine Childers ran a consignment of German arms into Howth, near Dublin, The Ulster Volunteers and the National Volunteers were facing one another, ready at any moment, it seemed, to fly at one another's throats, when the Great War intervened to avert the threat of the smaller one.

Irishmen, both Catholic and Protestant, flocked to the Colours. Redmond, the Irish Parliamentary leader, offered the National Volunteers for the defence of Ireland, and pledged them to 'join arms with the armed Protestant

Ulstermen' against the common enemy, but he was re-buffed. The Ulster Volunteers were given every aid and encouragement, and the promise that they would not be forced to accept Home Rule. The National Volunteers, in the South were denied arms and equipment and were shown, very clearly, that they were not considered reliable. As Lloyd George said, wise after the event two years later: 'Some of the—I want to get the right word—some of the stupidities which sometimes look almost like malignance, which were perpetrated at the beginning of recruiting in Ireland are beyond belief.' One of the unhappier recruiting slogans was: 'The trenches are safer than the Dublin slums.'

Parliament put Irish Home Rule into cold storage until a year after the end of the war, and turned its thoughts to the fight for little Belgium and the rights of small nationalities. In Ireland the Trade Union Congress and Labour Party denounced the war and discouraged recruiting. Behind it stood the autonomous Labour Force, the Irish Citizen Army which had been formed in the industrial troubles of 1913. It was, as Lenin said, the first Red Army in Europe, and it claimed that it served 'neither King George nor the Kaiser, but Ireland'. A minority broke away from the National Volunteers to form the Sinn Fein Irish Volunteers. They came under the control of the Irish Republican Brotherhood, for whom England's difficulty was traditionally Ireland's opportunity. Sir Roger Casement went to Germany in November, 1914, to secure support and arms for the cause of Irish independence. He was caught on landing in Ireland from a German submarine, and was tried and executed in England in 1916. The small but determined forces of the Irish Citizen Army and the Irish Volunteers drilled and trained for purposes other than National Defence and on Easter Monday, 1916, they struck.

The Easter Rebellion was a sadly mismanaged enterprise. The rebels proclaimed the Republic, occupied a number of buildings in Dublin and held out bravely for a week. A young mathematics teacher called de Valera was the last to surrender. There was little trouble in the rest of Ireland. The Irish people declined the nobly worded invitation 'to prove itself worthy of the august destiny to which it is called', and looting Dubliners made hay while the shells crashed and the bullets flew.

Never in the history of Ireland had a rebellion inspired so little sympathy. There were nearly a hundred thousand Catholic Irishmen fighting with the British Army, and the rebellion seemed as much a stab in the back to the majority of Irish people as it did to the English. The prisoners, who were marched through the streets, passed between lines of angry, jeering Dubliners. The cause of Irish independence seemed lost, or postponed to some far-distant date.

It needed an outstanding stroke of maladministration to revive Sinn Fein's fortunes. Sinn Fein had not been responsible for the rebellion which proved, however, to be its political beneficiary. The Dublin Castle authorities had been taken by surprise, and were as outraged as the men who, many years later, found that the amiable and apparently peaceful Kikuyu had turned into the dreadful Mau Mau. General Sir John Maxwell, the Commander of the British troops in Ireland, decided to teach the Irish a lesson they would never forget. He was to succeed beyond his expectations. He had fifteen rebel leaders shot. To rub the lesson home, the executions were spread over a number of days. James Connolly, the Socialist leader, who had been wounded in the fighting, was shot strapped to a chair.

Almost overnight men, whose names were unknown to most Irishmen, became glorious martyrs in the national cause, co-equal in the Roll of Honour with Wolfe Tone and Robert Emmett, who had challenged British power in 1798 and 1803. Ballads were composed in their honour. Yeats wrote 'A terrible beauty is born'. Post card photographs of *The Men Who Died* decorated thousands of homes all over the country, so that when the prisoners were released in 1917 they returned to a hero's welcome. It seems, at times, that an inescapable fate forced the English administration always to do the wrong thing in Ireland. 'Really it was only the usual childish petulance in which John Bull does things in a week that disgrace him for a century,' Bernard Shaw wrote 'though he soon recovers his good humour, and cannot understand why the survivors of his wrath do not feel as jolly with him as he does with them. On the smouldering ruins of Dublin the appeals to remember Louvain were presently supplemented by a fresh appeal. IRISHMEN: DO YOU WISH TO HAVE THE HORRORS OF WAR BROUGHT TO YOUR OWN HEARTHS AND HOMES? Dublin laughed sourly.' It is tempting but useless to speculate on what might have happened if the rebels had been amnestied and left to stew in their unpopularity. As it was, de Valera administered the first of many shocks three months later by winning a Sinn Fein electoral victory at East Clare on an openly Republican platform. In accordance with Sinn Fein policy, he did not take his seat at Westminster.

General Maxwell had established Sinn Fein firmly in the minds and hearts of many Irishmen, but it was left to another soldier, Sir Henry Wilson, the Chief of the Imperial General Staff, to crown his subordinate's work. In the spring of 1918, the shambles of the Western Front seemed likely to run short of cannon fodder. Sir Henry, a Southern Irishman with no sympathy for Home Rule or Republican aspirations, persuaded a reluctant Cabinet that Ireland was the nearest available source. The mere threat of conscription united the whole of Ireland against the British Government. The Roman Catholic Hierachy declared in the Bishops' Manifesto that the Irish people had 'a right to resist by every means that are consonant with the law of God'. A general strike called by the Irish Trade Union Congress and Labour Party closed all shops and factories, except those in Belfast, as a protest on the 23rd April—an inauspicious St. George's Day for Englishmen. Sinn Fein became the focus of the anti-conscription campaign, and attracted thousands of adherents from men of military age who, understandably, preferred to live in Ireland than to die in France.

Nevertheless, Lloyd George was still determined to put an Irish Conscription Bill on the Statute Book. In May, 1918, Field-Marshal Lord French was appointed Governor-General of Ireland to prepare the ground. Lloyd George impressed on him 'the necessity of putting the onus for first shooting on the rebels'. The good old veteran of the Boer War, who had been compensated with the title of Earl of Ypres after his removal from the command of the British Expeditionary Force early in the Great War, thought Ireland safe from a military point of view 'because aeroplanes, armoured cars, Maxims, etc., terrify the natives'.

Shortly after the arrival of the new Governor-General, Dublin Castle drew out of stock a trusty old weapon that often comes in handy in a difficult situation. It discovered a German plot. It was generally admitted to be a poor sample of its kind, but it served as an excuse to sweep hundreds of Sinn Feiners into gaol, and to intern, without charge or trial, the leaders of the movement, including de Valera and Arthur Griffith in England. This attempt to behead the movement of Irish Independence left the conduct of operations to two of the most resolute members of the Sinn Fein Executive still at large, the forty-four-year-old Cathal Brugha and the twenty-eight-year-old Michael Collins.

Both had fought and been taken prisoner in Easter Week. Brugha, *anglice* Charles Burgess, who no doubt inherited some of his stubborn pugnacity from his Yorkshire mother, was ablaze with the excessive zeal of the convert, and was prepared to shoot the Ministers responsible with his own hand if conscription were introduced in Ireland. He was saved from making the attempt, not by a change of heart at Westminster, but by the end of the war,

[16]

1. The Vanquished 1916: Prisoners of the Easter Rebellion are marched, unwept and unhonoured, through the streets of Dublin and down the Eden Quay to internment in England. The Irish cause seemed lost.

2. Conquering Heroes 1917: The same men were released a year later, and came home in triumph to find their names had been added to the national roll of glorious martyrs and rebels.

IRISHMEN AND IRISHWOMEN: In the name of God and of the dead generations from which she receives her old tradition of nationhood, Ireland, through us, summons her children to her flag and strikes for her freedom.

Having organised and trained her manhood through her secret revolutionary organisation, the Irish Republican Brotherhood, and through her open military organisations, the Irish Volunteers and the Irish Citizen Army, having patiently perfected her discipline, having resolutely waited for the right moment to reveal itself, she now seizes that moment, and, supported by her exiled children in America and by gallant allies in Europe, but relying in the first on her own strength, she strikes in full confidence of victory.

We declare the right of the people of Ireland to the ownership of Ireland, and to the unfettered control of Irish destinies, to be sovereign and indefeasible. The long usurpation of that right by a foreign people and government has not extinguished the right, nor can it ever be extinguished except by the destruction of the Irish people. In every generation the Irish people have asserted their right to national freedom and sovereignty; six times during the past three hundred years they have asserted it in arms. Standing on that fundamental right and again asserting it in arms in the face of the world, we hereby proclaim the Irish Republic as a Sovereign Independent State, and we pledge our lives and the lives of our comrades-in-arms to the cause of its freedom, of its welfare, and of its exaltation among the nations.

The Irish Republic is entitled to, and hereby claims, the allegiance of every Irishman and Irishwoman. The Republic guarantees religious and civil liberty, equal rights and equal opportunities to all its citizens, and declares its resolve to pursue the happiness and prosperity of the whole nation and of all its parts, cherishing all the children of the nation equally, and oblivious of the differences carefully fostered by an alien government, which have divided a minority from the majority in the past.

Until our arms have brought the opportune moment for the establishment of a permanent National Government, representative of the whole people of Ireland and elected by the suffrages of all her men and women, the Provisional Government, hereby constituted, will administer the civil and military affairs of the Republic in trust for the people.

We place the cause of the Irish Republic under the protection of the Most High God, Whose blessing we invoke upon our arms, and we pray that no one who serves that cause will dishonour it by cowardice, inhumanity, or rapine. In this supreme hour the Irish nation must, by its valour and discipline and by the readiness of its children to sacrifice themselves for the common good, prove itself worthy of the august destiny to which it is called.

Signed on Behalf of the Provisional Government,
THOMAS J. CLARKE.
SEAN Mac DIARMADA. THOMAS MacDONAGH.
P. H. PEARSE. EAMONN CEANNT.
JAMES CONNOLLY. JOSEPH PLUNKETT.

Reduced Facsimile of the Proclamation of the "Irish Republic"
Promulgated on Easter Sunday, 23rd April, 1916, at Liberty Hall, Dublin. The seven signatories to this document were all executed.

Cashman, Dublin.

3. Michael Collins in 1917: The soft-faced master of violence talks to a priest. Arthur Griffith the founder of Sinn Fein stands behind him.

4. This nobly worded appeal met with little response in 1916, but the execution of its seven signatories rallied Ireland to Sinn Fein.

5. Dangerous men: Arthur Griffith, twice deported and released; de Valera, sentenced to death and released, deported and escaped; Larry O'Neill, Lord Mayor of Dublin; Michael Collins, deported, released, and on the run, attend a sports meeting.

and turned his hand, instead, to the less spectacular task of building the Irish Republican Army out of the Volunteers who had joined up to avoid conscription. Brugha was an uncompromising militarist and republican, who doubled his duties as the Dáil's Minister of Defence with the management of the firm of ecclesiastical candlemakers. The majority of the volunteers had no more thought of fighting for Ireland than for England.

Michael Collins, as Director of Organisation and Intelligence began to spin an intelligence web involving sympathetic gaolers and policemen, workers in the Post Office, the railways and shipping lines. He was a member of the Supreme Council of the revolutionary Irish Republican Brotherhood which he had joined when he was working as a Post Office clerk in London, and less reluctant than many of the imprisoned leaders to accept the onus of shooting first. At a stormy meeting, well rigged by Irish Republican Brothers, he browbeat the Sinn Fein Executive into accepting the policy of creating general disorder as being the best means of achieving their aims: the seeds of violence were sown before Sinn Fein's electoral victory at the end of 1918. Collins was a natural organiser and conducted his campaign in a businesslike manner.

The political view from Dublin Castle steadily deteriorated during 1919. De Valera escaped from Lincoln Gaol in February and was elected President of the Dáil on his arrival in Ireland. The other prisoners were released in March. The Dáil set up its ministries and began to meet openly. It raised a public loan to finance its campaign for international recognition. The papers advertising it were suppressed, but the money began to pour into the concealed accounts opened by Michael Collins, who had become Minister of Finance, doubling the post with the office of Director of Organisation and Intelligence. These preparatory measures were accompanied by the first direct assault on the British Administration. The Dáil called upon the Irish people to boycott the Royal Irish Constabulary as agents of a foreign power.

This semi-military force, ten thousand strong, had been the Castle's executive arm for a century. A network of Constabulary barracks covered a country of poor communications and few large centres of population. The majority of Irish people still live in villages and hamlets of two hundred persons or less. The Constabulary kept the moonlighters, land-grabbers, cattle-rustlers and operators of poteen stills under control, and in small areas, where secrets are hard to keep, they knew what the local people were doing, and could often guess which peasant had been maliciously cutting off the tails of cows. The Sinn Fein boycott was aimed at the morale of this force. In the course of the campaign, decent and hitherto popular men were, at worst, brutally murdered by their compatriots, or at least treated as outcasts by their neighbours. Even worshippers at Mass ostentatiously avoided pews occupied by the police; tradesmen were afraid to deal with them; girls who walked out with the 'peelers' had their hair cut off. A party of bravos turned a constable's wife and children out of their house and burnt it. A woman had pig rings put into her buttocks for supplying milk to the police. Some hero, in a fit of rural idiocy, even stabbed and killed a donkey which carried turf to a police barracks.

These acts of hooliganism were not animated by the ideals of Sinn Fein. There was an ugly mood in the country. Ireland's chief export had for many years been people. Thousands of young men—one hundred thousand was Lord French's estimate—who would have emigrated but for the war, were stranded as displaced persons in their own country. Unemployment and low wages were general, and agrarian unrest was endemic in many areas. These conditions led to the first clashes with the police without the encouragement of the Sinn Fein boycott.

But as the year advanced the Volunteers of the young

Irish Republican Army began to make purposeful attacks. By the spring of 1919 Intelligence officers in the Castle could discern the pattern of a guerilla campaign emerging from the general disorder. Thinly held barracks were raided for arms and isolated policemen were ambushed or shot down in public places. Recruitment to the Royal Irish Constabulary all but stopped, and resignations began to reduce its numbers. In Dublin, Michael Collins was blunting another of the Administration's instruments by organising a band of dedicated assassins called 'the Squad' to terrorise the detectives of the 'G' Division, the Castle's Intelligence agency in the capital. The policeman's lot was not a happy one.

The officials at Dublin Castle, the administrative centre of the Government of Ireland and the accepted symbol of English oppression, were worried, but they did not appreciate the full extent of the threat to their authority. Sir John Taylor, the Assistant Under-Secretary, even thought that order could be restored by hitting the Irish in the pocket and put his faith in a measure making local councils financially liable for the disorder in their districts, at a time when one of the reasons for the trouble was that the trouble-makers had nothing in their pockets. This high Tory official was the man in charge. His superior, the Chief Secretary, McPherson, who had been appointed at the beginning of the year, spent more time at Westminster than in Dublin, and was reputed to go in fear of his life. The other Assistant Under-Secretary, J. MacMahon, had been appointed to placate the Church and Home Rulers because he was a Catholic with Nationalist sympathies, but then, for the same reasons, had been excluded from the conduct of affairs.

Taylor's imagination was bounded by the Castle walls, beyond which he could only move with an armed guard. He could remember the agrarian troubles thirty years before. He knew it all. No one could tell him about the constructive aims of Sinn Fein, or suggest a more promising policy than police and military raids and arrests. He concentrated all branches—finance, crime and appointments—in his own hands.

He also misinterpreted the way things were going and disastrously misinformed his masters at Westminster. Strikes, for example, in which Sinn Fein and Unionist employers usually united against Sinn Fein workers, seemed to him to show a fatal division in the Sinn Fein ranks. Police reports that terrorism, cattle-rustling and highway robbery were spreading over the countryside suggested that Sinn Fein farmers and shopkeepers might be thinking again in some areas. There was also, on precedent, every reason to suppose that this Irish rebellion would be betrayed by traitors, as had all the others, and be easily crushed.

Sinn Fein certainly had its difficulties, but the state of Ireland at Midsummer in 1919 scarcely supported the hope that it would perish of its own contradictions. Its delegates went to Versailles to enlist the sympathy of President Wilson at the Peace Conference. The President had promised a settlement by which 'every people should choose its own master', but told the discouraged Irishmen: 'You have touched on the great metaphysical tragedy of today. My words have roused hopes in the hearts of millions of people. . . . When I gave utterance to those words, I said them without the knowledge that nationalities existed which are coming to us today.' The President had, of course, heard of Ireland, but assumed, like most other people, Irishmen included, that the country was as much a part of the United Kingdom as Wales or Scotland. This failure had only made the Volunteers feel that they stood on their own, and so spurred them to further violence. The President of the Dáil, de Valera, had secretly left for the United States to raise money and to mobilise public opinion on their behalf. The Volunteers, or the Irish Republican Army, as they now came to be known, were clearly emerging in the Castle reports as a force at war with the Crown. For the first time in Irish history the Castle authorities found it difficult, but not impossible, to hire informers.

In Dublin, soldiers in steel helmets patrolled the streets with fixed bayonets. Searches by military raiding parties reminded newspaper correspondents of the German occupation of Belgium, though some remarked upon the extreme youth of most of the soldiery. The tanks, armoured cars, lorries, guns and other military stores which were unloaded on the quays certainly suggested that an expeditionary force was being equipped against some formidable enemy; but the British Army was not at war with the few hundred poorly-armed shop assistants and farm boys of the I.R.A. who began to raid police barracks more boldly.

The object of these attacks was to obtain the arms and ammunition that were needed to extend the struggle. Constables who surrendered were released. These actions had some of the excitement of war for those who had missed the real thing, but few of its dangers. The barracks had not been designed as fortresses, and could easily be attacked and often set on fire from neighbouring houses and shops, and the constables were always heavily outnumbered. In August one police barracks was destroyed in County Cork, and another in County Clare. Two constables were killed and one wounded in these engagements. The Royal Irish Constabulary began to withdraw its men from outlying areas and to concentrate them in larger and more defensible units.

The ordinary processes of law were collapsing in Cork County, where witnesses refused to give evidence for fear of attack by I.R.A. gunmen, and in County Clare Sinn Fein established its own police and law courts. The Castle administration was beginning to crumble, and worse was to come. British soldiers, up to this point, had enjoyed a close season; they had behaved on the whole with restraint, and had been treated with respect. But on Sunday, the

7th September, a unit of the No. 2 Cork Brigade I.R.A., under the command of Liam Lynch, shot up a party of the King's Shropshire Light Infantry on their way to church parade at the Wesleyan chapel at Fermoy. They killed one soldier, wounded four and disarmed the bemused remainder before leaping into their cars and driving away.

At the inquest the next day, the Coroner described this engagement as 'an act of actual warfare', adding, in the hyperbolic idiom, commonly used to describe I.R.A. actions, 'it would take a military strategy of the highest order to equal it'. The jury refused to return a verdict of murder and found that the deceased had died from a bullet wound 'fired by some person unknown'. Two hundred soldiers invaded the town in the evening and wrecked the shops of the tradesmen who had been on the jury and some others, causing in all £3,000 damage. The events at Fermoy established a pattern of attack and reprisal that was to become sadly familiar. Three days later the Castle suppressed Dáil Eireann and thereby, as Arthur Griffith said with justifiable exaggeration, 'proclaimed the whole of the Irish nation as an illegal assembly'. Throughout the autumn the Crown Forces carried out raids and searches, broke up political, cultural and sports meetings, dismantled printing presses and made arrests on a scale large enough to anger the Irish people, cause dismay across the Irish Sea and fury on the other side of the Atlantic. The British Ambassador to Washington reported, at the end of the year, that he was 'almost powerless for good owing to the universal sentiment in favour of Ireland'.

Dáil Eireann continued to meet clandestinely, but the conduct of affairs passed increasingly to the Irish Republican Army and particularly into the hands of Michael Collins, its Director of both Organisation and Intelligence. His photograph appeared in the police journal, *Hue and Cry*, with the warning: 'A dangerous man. Care should be taken that he does not fire first.'

The I.R.A. used the autumn for consolidation and training. *The Times* correspondent might think that 'the prospect of dying for Ireland haunts the dreams of thousands of youths today', but it seemed different on the spot. Ernie O'Malley, one of the most devoted and gifted of Irish patriots who was organising North County Dublin complained, in a despatch of the 19th December, 1919, of 'lack of spirit on the part of the men, lack of knowledge on the part of the officers'. The romantic Dan Breen, the man who had fired the first shots at Soloheadbeg, reported later that 'we were burdened with thousands of recruits who were not in their hearts in favour of any stronger weapon than resolutions'.

The Irish people had voted for Sinn Fein, but not for war against England. At the General Election they had chosen, they imagined, an unspecified policy of passive resistance combined with a 'Buy Irish Goods' campaign. The men who wanted action were, as in most rebellions and revolutions, a very small minority. They were determined to make things worse in order to make them better. In an attempt to force the pace, Dan Breen and ten other Volunteers tried to ambush and assassinate Lord French, the Viceroy, on the 19th December. The intelligence and planning by Michael Collins had been good, but the execution was badly bungled. One of the essential members of this party was having a jar of stout as the vice-regal car sped by, and before he had wiped the froth from his lips the assailants had lost one of their number and Breen himself been wounded. They meant to kill the Viceroy on principle, it was explained later, not because they disliked him. They were emulating, perhaps, the assassins who had killed Lord Frederick Cavendish, the Chief Secretary for Ireland, and Burke, the Permanent Under-Secretary, in Phoenix Park in 1882. 'We did it to make history,' one of the assailants said on that occasion.

At Westminster, Lloyd George was keeping Ireland in

the back, rather than the front, of his mind. His Government was beset with many problems—strikes and unemployment at home, military and diplomatic crises abroad. The Sinn Fein demand for an independent Republic left no room for negotiation. The I.R.A., in its first year of war against England, had killed at most twenty-six people, eighteen of them policemen, and had fired shots in anger at human targets, or at buildings, on not much more than a hundred occasions.

No government could capitulate to such a threat. At that time the Dervishes in Somaliland were giving a more troublesome account of themselves, in their own wild way, under a leader known as 'Mad Mullah'. The position in Egypt, Mesopotamia and India was much more menacing. British troops were involved in an unfortunate military adventure in Russia, and were standing-by in Germany, Constantinople and Syria. Empires had fallen, great events were impending and Ireland was making a bad situation worse by tying up men who were needed elsewhere.

So, at a time when he was largely preoccupied with other anxieties, Lloyd George outlined his proposals for an optimistically entitled 'Better Government of Ireland' Bill to the House of Commons on the 22nd December, and announced the Government's intention to partition the country and set up two governments. His proposals interested Irishmen no more than had the original Irish Home Rule Act. But in the New Year of 1920 the tortuous course of Anglo-Irish history took a new turn: the first volunteers to answer a Press advertisement for men prepared to 'face a rough and dangerous task' were recruited for the Royal Irish Constabulary at specially opened offices in Glasgow and Liverpool. Their destination was Ireland where, three months later, they were to win a place in Irish legend and history as the 'Black and Tans'.

CHAPTER TWO

Patriots v. Peelers

THE ANGLO-IRISH officials in Dublin Castle were honest, tradition-bound, notoriously incompetent and without real power or authority. Their masters were in London. They could do nothing but continue their efforts to crush the rival government which sought to usurp their place.

At the beginning of 1920 the prisons were filling up, and many members of the Dáil, Sinn Fein, the Volunteers, the Trade Union Congress and Labour Party were on the run. With warrants out for their arrest, they never slept at home and rarely spent two successive nights in the same house. Raids and round-ups became a commonplace in Dublin and Cork, and terror began to sour the happy-go-lucky temperament of the most unpolitical Irishmen. The rattle of tanks and armoured cars at night, the rap of a rifle butt on the door with the command to open-up, disturbed the rest of Unionists and Republicans alike. Both had to give a good account of themselves, or be taken away for further questioning. Soldiers searched for guns and documents through bedding, women's clothes in wardrobes, under mattresses and carpets and up chimneys, while frightened and often abusive men, women and children stood by in their night clothes. In daytime whole areas were cordoned off by tanks and armoured cars, while troops went in with fixed bayonets to search the district, street by street and house by house. Although the military nearly always performed their unpleasant duty with restraint, punctiliously paying for any damage, they hardly endeared themselves to Irish hearts. Two hundred and twenty arrests were made in the first month of the year.

The British Army, 43,000 strong, was neither at war nor strictly neutral. In normal times it used Ireland as a training ground, and the presence of British troops in the country had no political significance: even in these troubled times it was not an Army of Occupation, as Sinn Fein liked to call it. No part of the country was under martial law, and the Army's activity was limited to helping the Civil Power maintain law and order.

The Volunteers of the Irish Republican Army suffered from no such restrictions. They continued their war against England by raiding for arms and attacking their compatriots in the Royal Irish Constabulary. Two constables were wounded on the 2nd January. Four barracks were attacked on the 4th, another on the 5th. On the 6th January the prisoners in Cork gaol began a hunger strike. The Volunteers had borrowed this weapon from the English Suffragettes, and a Republican veteran, Thomas Ashe, had already died after forcible feeding in 1917 to make another martyr in the national cause.

On the 8th the home of a J.P. was raided in Bodyke, County Clare, and a number of sporting rifles and revolvers were seized. On the next day a large party of Volunteers attacked Castlehackett R.I.C. Barracks, but were routed by a couple of constables who took them in the rear. The eminent Irish barrister, Sergeant Sullivan, K.C., who had defended Sir Roger Casement, also had his left eyebrow singed by one of the shots fired at him by a band of armed men in Tralee, but this was said to be the work of criminals.

'The state of Ireland is terrible,' Field-Marshal Sir Henry Wilson, the Chief of the Imperial General Staff, wrote in his diary on 13th January. 'Spies and murderers everywhere; the Cabinet absolutely apathetic. I urge with all my force the necessity for doubling the police and not employing the military.' The Cabinet could be excused for not taking the I.R.A.'s war effort very seriously. There was a lull in Irish hostilities for the mid-January Municipal elections in which Sinn Fein secured a large majority on a Proportional Representation vote. Analysis of the figures, however, showed an anti-Sinn Fein majority if the first preference votes alone were considered. At this stage Sinn Fein was far from having the whole-hearted popular support for its declaration of independence which the figures suggested. The Unionists, who were in favour of the British connection, were down, but far from out. The Trade Union Congress, with a quarter of a million members, was conducting its own independent, but parallel, campaign for self-determination. It had rejected a Sinn Fein recommendation to sever its connections with British Trade Unions, and, if it came to the point, some of its leaders preferred the British Monarchy to the prospect of an Irish bourgeois Republic. At the time when the Irish delegation sought recognition at the Versailles Peace Conference, Thomas Johnson and Cathal O'Shannon had already attended the Labour and Socialist International at Berne and returned with the report that: 'We have grown still stronger in our conviction that the Soviet Government is Ireland's best and most disinterested friend, and that, at least so far as justice and principle are concerned, the Labour and Socialist Governments are our only hope, and our only friends among the Governments.' They looked farther than Sinn Fein, both abroad and at home, where their policy included winning 'for workers an ever-increasing share of the produce of their combined labour, until the present system which gives the control of industry to those who live upon rent, interest and profit, is abolished'.

The active members of the I.R.A. did not even enjoy the support of the majority of Sinn Fein for their glorious struggle for independence. They knew it, but they did not mind. 'It was madness but glorious madness,' as the O'Rahilly had declared in the 1916 rising. They were inspired by the partly legendary story of ancient wrongs and the determination to clear the English, and English Administration, out of the island. They were fighting for twenty acres for every man, for a land peopled by saints and scholars, where art and industry would flourish and give Ireland her rightful place in the forefront of the nations. All that separated them from this earthly paradise was the Union with Great Britain. This apparent truth was always, and has since been proved to be, a sad delusion. The emotion was nevertheless genuine. Were not Brian Boru, Queen Tailtu, Roderick O'Connor, Parnell and de Valera with them against Strongbow, Cromwell and Lloyd George?

Such nationalist sentiments have always seemed strange to the English who have had little cause to feel them, but they have been shared by many peoples in different parts of the world. The best of the I.R.A. were the passionate idealists for whom the means justified the end; the worst merely demonstrated the Irish peasant's callous indifference to the sanctity of human life, a characteristic which the dramatist, J. M. Synge, had pointed out to the distress of the Sinn Feiners who had shouted down the first performance of *The Playboy of the Western World* with cries of 'Up Sinn Fein'.

The attacks on barracks, mostly unsuccessful, continued. A constable was mortally wounded in Thurles on the 20th January, and the R.I.C. hit back, for the first time that year, by breaking eleven panes of glass in the Sinn Fein Hall, smashing two shop windows and firing a number of volleys down the street as a reprisal. No one was hurt. This outbreak was described as the 'sacking of Thurles'. On the next day in Dublin, Michael Collins' 'Squad' struck its most effective blow against the Castle's detective force by assassinating Assistant Commissioner Redmond, of the Dublin Metropolitan Police, in Grafton Street. He had been on his way to his hotel from his office in the Castle. The Castle authorities offered £10,000 reward for evidence to convict the offenders in the murders of Redmond, four other detectives of the Dublin Metropolitan Police and nine officers and men of the Royal Irish Constabulary. They also offered £1,000 for secret information, and £10,000 for the body of Michael Collins, dead or alive.

Sinn Fein struck another blow, this time at the prestige of the Castle, by electing Alderman Tom Kelly, a prisoner in Wormwood Scrubs, Lord Mayor of Dublin. The Castle replied by making sixty-five arrests in a country-wide round up, using both the police and the military, and on the 5th February imposed a curfew in Dublin from midnight to 5 a.m.

The Irish Republican Army, which made such drastic measures necessary, was estimated by Lord French, the Viceroy, to be about 100,000 strong. This was an alarming exaggeration. The Secretary for Ireland went further, and spoke of a Sinn Fein army of 200,000 men, 'ready to murder by day and night'. The strength of the I.R.A. on paper, seems, in fact, never to have exceeded 15,000, and its effective strength, according to Michael Collins, Director of Intelligence, was 'not more than three thousand fighting men'. The tactical unit was the company of seventy-six to a hundred men. Four to seven companies made a battalion and three to six battalions a brigade. The supreme authority was the General Headquarters Staff in Dublin, which co-ordinated and directed the Army operations, but which had, necessarily, to rely largely upon the initiative of the local commanders. *An t-Oglac*, at first the bi-monthly and later weekly official organ of the Irish Volunteers, provided exhortation and training notes in about equal measure to all units and was clandestinely circulated in flour sacks and other disguises. Women and auxiliaries were organised in the *Cumann na m'Ban*, or Irishwomen's Council, and boys in the *Fianna Eireann*, described as the Irish National Boy Scouts Association. 'Boys! Ireland is calling you,' a recruiting leaflet reads. 'Boys! Join the young army of Ireland which has already given so many martyrs to the cause of Irish Independence, and help to win the crown of freedom for your Motherland.' These were the forces of the Republic.

The young army of Ireland had, fortunately, given very few martyrs to the cause, and was at no time called upon to make great sacrifices in the field. As Dr. Cohalan, Bishop of Cork, observed in a pastoral letter condemning the I.R.A. attacks on the Royal Irish Constabulary, 'ambushers take very little risk to themselves'. Neither did the Volunteers who attacked barracks. One hundred and twenty men, for example, were mobilised for the capture of the Ballytrain R.I.C. post in County Monaghan on St. Valentine's Day. It was a semi-detached building manned by six constables. They only surrendered after a gable end had been demolished by gelignite, which the I.R.A. jocularly called *Bas gan Sagart* or 'Death without the priest'. Six carbines, a Very light pistol and a quantity of ammunition were captured in this operation, which was celebrated in a popular ballad of the time.

> That day of renown
> When the rebels of Monaghan they all gathered around
> The leaders addressed them and men of great fame
> When an order was issued to attack Ballytrain.

Every Irishman is proverbially something of a poet.

On the same night raiders for arms shot a farmer's wife who was defending herself with a spade in Enniscorthy. It was here that the Chairman of the Urban District Council had struck another blow for the cause a few days earlier, by tearing the record of a resolution, condemning the Easter Week rising, out of the Council Minute Book. In a successful coup in Holycross a constable was stripped naked and the woman with him had her head cropped to make another incident, in what the I.R.A. Chief of Staff, Richard Mulcahy, called 'the finest annals of any army in history'. The gunmen who shot two constables returning from Mass in Toomevara were also, in a small way, helping, in de Valera's words, 'to break the chain which binds our sweet, sad mother'. In a St. Patrick's Day message from New York 'to the sons and daughters of Gael wherever you may be', he declared 'it is still our duty to show the world the might of moral beauty'.

Though the I.R.A. could not live up to its military pretensions, it put the police on the defensive. Their barracks might be attacked at any time of the day or night. They were in constant fear of death by ambush or assassination at the hands of their neighbours and their families were persecuted. In these circumstances it is surprising that only a minority resigned. Barracks and Court houses were abandoned in the remoter parts of the south and west of the country, where the King's writ was ceasing to run. At the March Assizes in North Tipperary, for example, there were only three trivial cases for trial, though the list of indictable offences reported by the police included two murders, two attempted murders, three cases of wounding, four cases of robbery and attempts to rob, three cases of arson, three of killing or maiming cattle, thirteen of malicious injury, four raids for arms and two attacks on barracks. Judges had similar experiences in other parts of the country.

In a large part of the south and west the Sinn Fein police, young men with green armlets, kept what order there was, and the Sinn Fein Courts administered their own rough justice with variable, and sometimes impressive success. They had no easy task. The countryside was in a state of ferment. Land was being seized right and left, and cattle-driving becoming a commonplace. A landowner was driven naked through a crowded fair in Roscommon. One Galway landlord was shot and another ducked in a pond until he agreed to his tenants' demands. Private vengeance could be given a respectable, patriotic gloss by pinning on to the clothes of the corpse the notice: 'Spies and informers beware.' Ordinary criminals, leaving the towns for the countryside, added to the increasing chaos.

Meanwhile, public opinion in England became restive. Between January, 1919, and March, 1920, there were over twenty thousand raids on houses by the Crown Forces in Ireland, nearly four hundred political arrests and deportations, four hundred and twenty-nine proclamations to suppress meetings and newspapers, and the end was not in sight. A Labour Party mission, which had gone to Ireland early in 1920, reported, temperately enough, on the 20th. February, that 'much of the prevailing discontent is unquestionably to be attributed to the methods of the present administration'.

The Irish were also beginning to make themselves felt in England. Arthur Griffith came over to London to address a mass protest meeting at the Albert Hall on the 8th February. To add interest to this occasion, Mrs. Despard, the Viceroy's sister, was on the platform. In March, William O'Brien, the Secretary of the Irish Trade Union Congress and Labour Party, who was then a prisoner in Wormwood Scrubs, was nominated by the local Irish in the Stockport by-election because they were dissatisfied with the British Labour Executive's attitude to Irish independence. Cathal O'Shannon, an Irish Labour man also 'on the run', was his election agent. The Irish Trade Union and Labour Executive had not authorised this nomination, but it was, as they said, 'a useful piece of propaganda.'

At Westminster Parliament debated the Bill 'For the Better Government of Ireland'. In Ireland it was known more simply as the 'Partition Bill'. It provided for two Parliaments, one for the six counties of Antrim, Armagh, Down, Fermanagh, Derry and Tyrone in the North, and another for the twenty-six counties in the South. Matters excluded from their jurisdiction included the Crown, the making of peace and war, treaties and foreign relations, and the Navy, Army and Air Force. The Bill also proposed

6. A military round-up in O'Connell Street: Scenes such as this were common in Dublin, which, in 1920 was as much a part of the United Kingdom as London, Edinburgh or Cardiff.

7. The most respectable citizens were stopped and searched for arms and papers by young soldiers. All Irishmen were potential Sinn Feiners. This bicyclist might have been Michael Collins for all they knew.

8. Soldiers with fixed bayonets restrain an unintimidated crowd of onlookers during a police and military round-up. Scenes like this reminded newspaper correspondents of the German occupation of Belgium.

9. Motorists had to carry passes and were halted at the approaches to the bigger towns. Michael Collins, who had a £10,000 price on his head, dead or alive, frequently underwent this scrutiny.

a Council of Ireland which was to co-ordinate the administration of the two Governments, and could, as one of its
first acts, proclaim the Union of Ireland and set up a single
Parliament for the whole country. Members of both
Parliaments were required to take an oath of allegiance
to the Crown. If a majority of either Parliament refused to
take the oath, the Parliament in question would be dissolved
and the part of Ireland it represented would be administered
by the Lord-Lieutenant and a committee of the Privy
Council. The Bill was coolly received: in the Republican
South because Ireland was one and indivisible, in Loyalist
Ulster because it would sever the six counties from the
United Kingdom.

Partition pleased almost nobody and the gerrymandering
problem of carving a Protestant state out of the North,
where there was a large catholic element which favoured
the South, was formidable; but it appeared to many to
make the best of a bad job. Even if the original plantation
of Scots settlers in Northern Ireland had been the historical
crime that Irish nationalists claimed, it had taken root,
and in the course of time developed its own distinctive
characteristics. Lloyd George did not wickedly invent the
bigoted Protestant frenzy of the Orangeman, or his determined refusal to submit to a government in Dublin. The
passionate loyalty which could be expressed by firing at
soldiers of the Norfolk Regiment because the Duke of
Norfolk was a Catholic had certainly not been made in
England. If the British Government had recognised Dáil
Eireann and withdrawn its forces from Ireland, it would
have exposed the country to the certainty of civil war
between North and South, with the danger of intervention
of the kind that occurred later in the Spanish Civil War of
1936–38.

The Ulster Unionists decided to accept the Bill with some
reservations, but the Republicans in the South could only
reflect that the North had secured Partition by the threat

of force in 1914 and that they might win a united Ireland by imitation. The political impasse was complete. There is not usually an easy exit from a bad situation and often no way of avoiding the road from bad to worse.

In Cork, the murder of Lord Mayor MacCurtain on the 19th March suggested that the worst was yet to come. On that night a party of armed men with blackened faces knocked on the door of the Lord Mayor's house. He was in bed and his wife opened the door. They brushed past her, went upstairs and called on him to come out. As he opened his bedroom door they opened fire with their revolvers and mortally wounded him. This murder raised outrage to a new level. As *The Irish Times* observed editorially: 'That the chief citizen of one of our great cities should be shot in his own house, and that his murderers should escape, provide a terrible commentary on the state of this unhappy island.' It did indeed, and more particularly as the police had committed the murder. Murder is murder, whoever does the killing, but it is perhaps worse if it is committed by the forces of law and order, even under provocation. The death of MacCurtain caused a sensation in Ireland. Few people believed the official report that the Mayor had been killed by his own side for not having been active enough as the Commandant of the Mid-Cork Brigade of the I.R.A. Similar suggestions were repeated in later cases, but were hardly ever convincing. The word of Michael Collins is to be preferred. He was convinced that Divisional Inspector Swanzy, of the Royal Irish Constabulary, had led the murder party, and even Loyalists like Sir James O'Connor, a Lord Justice of Appeal, were in no doubt that the police were the culprits. Collins had Swanzy shot in Northern Ireland later in the year, and the rest of the party as and when opportunity offered. At the inquest on MacCurtain the jury added a note of farce to a grim business by bringing in a verdict of murder against the Prime Minister, the Viceroy and the Inspector-General of the R.I.C., as well as against D. I. Swanzy and some unknown constables.

There was no argument about who murdered a septuagenarian Resident Magistrate, Alan Bell, the following week in Dublin. This murder was openly admitted to be another blow against the might of England. The old gentleman was travelling by tram from his home to his office in Dublin Castle, where he was investigating the links between certain Irish banks and the Sinn Fein organisation. At one of the stops, half a dozen young men boarded the tram. One of them tapped him on the shoulder and said: 'Come on, Mr. Bell, your time has come.' They dragged him into the road and shot him dead with revolvers. No one tried to stop the assailants.

These two murders set the pattern of the so-called Anglo-Irish war. It consisted of a number of small violent incidents which would have gone unnoticed in a general war. Only very rarely did the number of killed or wounded in any engagement go into two figures. The acts of aggression were numerous enough to disturb, but never to entirely disrupt the ordinary, everyday life of going to work, shopping, drinking, talking and spending a day at the races. Dinner was served as usual in many Unionist houses but with a revolver laid in each place as an addition to the cutlery. At worst, life was lived in the shadow of apprehension as though in a city exposed to the occasional attacks of not very lethal flying bombs. The monthly casualties were mercifully small and, although impossible to determine exactly, were probably about twice the number of people who are killed and injured on the roads of Ireland today. Imaginations which had been stunned by the fearful slaughter of the Great War could more easily recognise the ugly face of violence when it was brought down to this small scale. Most of the killing by both sides had the squalid interest of a murder in a back street. Every incident made news, as the Sinn Fein propagandists were quick to realise.

Newspaper readers on the other side of the Irish Channel could not help knowing, and being shocked by, some of the things that were done in their name. Such was the Irish setting for the first English recruits to the Royal Irish Constabulary who arrived on the 25th March, 1920. Five days later they were greeted with a proclamation which was posted throughout the South of Ireland:

1. Whereas the spies and traitors known as the Royal Irish Constabulary are holding this country for the enemy, and whereas said spies and bloodhounds are conspiring with the enemy to bomb and bayonet and otherwise outrage a peaceful, law-abiding, and liberty-loving people;

2. Wherefore we do hereby proclaim and suppress said spies and traitors, and do hereby solemnly warn prospective recruits that they join the R.I.C. at their own peril. All nations are agreed as to the fate of traitors. It has the sanction of God and man.

By order of the G.O.C.
Irish Republican Army.

The 'Tan War', as it came to be known in Ireland, had been declared.

CHAPTER THREE

New Tools for an Old Job

THE ENGLISH RECRUITS to the Royal Irish Constabulary who disembarked at North Wall dock in Dublin were a tough-looking crowd. Their appearance hardly suggested that they had been selected, as Winston Churchill said, 'from a great press of applicants on account of their intelligence, their characters, and their records in the war'. Yet they were not the sweepings of the English gaols as Irish propagandists claimed, but rather the heroes who had fought in the famous 'war to end all wars' and survived to live without a job in Lloyd George's 'land fit for heroes'. Many of them were certainly demoralised. 'Hardly a week passes now,' Bernard Shaw wrote, 'without some soldier who braved death in the field so recklessly that he was decorated or specially commended for it, being hailed before our magistrates for having failed to resist the paltriest temptations of peace, with no better excuse than the old one that "a man must live".' They were of the same breed as the Unknown Soldier who, safely dead, was to be buried with great pomp in Westminster Abbey later in the year.

The advertised wage of ten shillings a day and all found was a princely sum in the troubled and hungry 'twenties. There was no shortage of applicants, but there were not enough of the dark green R.I.C. uniforms with which to clothe them They were equipped with khaki service dress supplemented with constabulary uniform, and appeared in a strange medley of khaki and dark green, some in khaki tunic and green trousers, others in khaki alone, some with civilian hats, but most with the green caps and black leather belts of the R.I.C. When they appeared in Limerick they were promptly nicknamed the 'Black and Tans' after a once-famous pack of hounds. They never looked or behaved like policemen. Their only service experience had been in trench warfare which had a brutalising rather than ennobling effect, a training quite useless against the Irish Republican Army's tip-and-run campaign. Their morale had not been improved by months of unemployment. The Army had taught them that the reputation for a good character can be based on undiscovered crime and that scrounging only becomes stealing if it is found out. They were used to the graded punishments of military discipline, but the R.I.C. officers under whom they now served had no such powers over them. The ultimate threat of dismissal, the policeman's most serious punishment, had no terror for men who had joined up in an emergency and who were not embarking on a career with pension rights. Ineffective discipline and an addiction to the native pastime of swilling stout and the wine of the country soon produced the men who caused a Unionist Limerick landowner to exclaim: 'These blackguards should never have been let loose in this country. They are not gentlemen.' They were not, and by their ungentlemanly behaviour over a few short months made it very difficult for any Irishman to remain neutral in the struggle against England.

The full force of Black and Tan violence and indiscipline did not break out until later in the year. At first their curious rig even made them popular curiosities in many parts of the country. Meanwhile other changes were made in the administration of Ireland. On the 23rd March Lloyd George offered General Sir Nevil Macready, then Commissioner of the Metropolitan Police, the command of the forces in Ireland. The Prime Minister told Sir Nevil that he thought his experience of police work would help to co-ordinate the activities of the military and police in Ireland. Macready's experience included the command of police and troops in times of civil disorder during the bitter South Wales coal strikes of 1910, and he had more recently dealt successfully with the London police strike of 1919. He accepted the post Lloyd George offered him with some misgiving, having acquired a distaste for Irish politics in general and Ulster in particular when, in 1914, Mr. Asquith sent him from the War Office to deal with the crisis caused in the island by the Home Rule Bill. 'The deciding factor, indeed the only one that weighed with me,' he wrote later, 'was the evident desire of my old chief, Lord French, that I should take the appointment. But for that nothing would have induced me to return to a country to which I was never attracted, or to take up a task which I instinctively felt would be affected by every variation of the political weathercock, and in which it was doubtful if any satisfactory result could be obtained.' On the 1st April Ian Macpherson resigned the office of Chief Secretary to Ireland, and was succeeded two days later by Sir Hamar Greenwood, K.C., Liberal M.P. for Sunderland and Under-Secretary to the Home Office. This bluff Welsh Canadian had, for some time, been anxious to rush into the place where others feared to tread. He was a forthright and vigorous man who had much of the assurance of the fairground barker that he had once been before coming to England to read for the Bar. He could speak well to a prepared brief, but his extemporisations were less happy. In some parts of Ireland it soon became the habit to say of any tall story 'don't tell a Greenwood'.

The day of his appointment was the Saturday before Easter. Dublin Castle expected another rising on the anniversary of the 1916 rebellion. Troops established check points on the main roads into Dublin, Cork and Limerick and searched all cars. The expected attack did not come, but in the evening, just before curfew, groups of young men called at nearly a hundred income tax offices all over the country, from Belfast to Cork, firmly escorted the official and his family from the house, piled all the tax books and other documents on the floor, soaked the premises in paraffin and set them on fire. Later in the night the Volunteers burned one hundred and eighty-two evacuated police barracks to prevent their reoccupation by the reinforced Constabulary. The Castle was taken completely off guard.

Both these operations were well planned and executed on a countrywide scale. They proved, as Lord French observed in an interview, that while the I.R.A. showed no evidence of any military brains, there was no doubt of its great organising power. 'Two morals are drawn from Saturday's deliberate and successful raids,' *The Times* commented editorially on Easter Monday. 'The first is that the Republican movement has become a really serious menace to British authority. The other, that the Government must devise better methods of combating the campaign.'

British opinion received another shock when eighty political prisoners started a hunger strike in Mountjoy gaol, where they had been detained from periods ranging from weeks to months without trial. At the end of a week many prisoners were in a serious condition. The Castle sent telegrams to the relatives telling them that a son, husband or brother was dying, and bidding them to come quickly. They came from all over Ireland. The scenes inside the gaol were harrowing. The approaches to Mountjoy were blocked with crowds of sympathisers and sightseers. They pressed against the tanks and the steel-helmeted soldiers who stood on guard with fixed bayonets. The photographs and reports in the newspapers made shocking reading at British breakfast tables. Many members of all parties pressed the Government to release the prisoners, but received an apparently unyielding reply from Mr. Bonar Law, the Leader of the House: 'The Government consider it their duty, as had been done over and over again when Ireland was in a similar condition, to arrest men on suspicion in

order to prevent crime. We have done so, and we feel it our
duty to continue to do so, and it would be perfectly futile
to do it if men are to be released because they choose to
refuse food. This decision has been taken by His Majesty's
Government and I do not believe there is any chance of
altering it.' Later, he added, 'There is no possibility of a
change of attitude of the Government in the matter. The
Government has counted the cost.' This answer had logic, if
not humanity, but his confidence was falsified by events.
On the 12th April, Thomas Farren, the Chairman, and
Thomas Johnson, the Acting Secretary of the Irish T.U.C.
and Labour Party, called a general strike. Their proclamation once more emphasised Labour's independent power:
'Workers of Ireland: You are called upon to act swiftly and
suddenly to save a hundred dauntless men. At this hour
their lives are hanging by a thread in a Bastille. These men—
for the greater part our fellow workers and comrades in
our trade unions—have been forcibly taken from their
homes and their families and imprisoned without charge, or,
if charged, tried under exceptional laws for alleged offences
of a political character, in outrageous defiance to every
canon of justice . . . .Workers: Let your response to this
sudden call be so unanimous as will impress the people of
other lands with your determination to put an end to
tyranny and oppression. Irish workers, in the name of
humanity, give a lead in this as you did in your fight against
conscription!' Once more the call to strike shut down
industry and commerce all over the country, except in
Belfast. Workers' Committees organised the food supply
and many town councils lent their municipal buildings. The
strike demonstrated both Irish Labour's discipline and
influence and the division between North and South. The
Standing Committee of the Roman Catholic Hierarchy
allied itself with popular feeling and placed the moral
responsibility of anything that might happen on 'the
Government that substitutes cruelty, vengeance and gross

injustice for the equity, moderation and fair play which should ever accompany the exercise of repressive law. The cry we utter today is the cry of humanity.' Ireland had not been so unitedly opposed to the Dublin Castle administration since the campaign against conscription in 1917.

General Macready arrived to take up his command on the second day of the general strike to find Dublin at a standstill and the streets crowded with people excitedly discussing the hunger strike. At the end of a day of agitated discussion at the Viceregal Lodge, Lord French decided to release all the prisoners who had been arrested under the Defence of the Realm Regulations, but not those against whom a charge had been preferred. The first prisoner to be discharged was a petty criminal who had been sentenced by the Recorder of Dublin. 'After this it seemed hopeless to expect that the simplest administrative action could be taken without somebody bungling.' General Macready observed. In the next forty-eight hours he was appalled at the chaos in Dublin Castle, caused largely by Sir John Taylor's passion for centralising everything in his own hands. With the Viceroy's permission, he wrote to London to ask if a small committee of experts might be sent to reorganise the Administration as the first step towards, what Sir Henry Wilson called, 'stamping out the rebellion with a strong hand'.

The general strike was called off after the release of the hunger strikers. Three more members of the Royal Irish Constabulary were killed during the excitements, and three others in the course of the next few days; a British soldier was killed and several civilians received bayonet wounds in an affray at Limerick, and in another at Arklow young soldiers, who were being taunted by the crowd, took the law into their own hands and shot one civilian and wounded another. General Macready thought, strangely, that 'occurrences such as this had a most soothing effect on the locality where they happened', but added, 'however much one may have sympathy with the troops, knowing that the populace was baiting them with the hopes of retaliation, it was, of course, essential to nip such proceedings in the bud.' Drunken Black and Tans beat up civilians and smashed windows in Limerick as a foretaste of worse to come on the 28th April. Disturbances of this kind were, however, sporadic and scattered. There were days of quiet unshattered by the crack of a single rifle, and in fourteen of Ireland's thirty-two counties no shot had been fired since the beginning of the year, and in most there had been no more than one or two raids for arms on private houses. As *An t-Oglach*, the Volunteer journal, reported on the 1st May, 'those places where guerilla warfare against the enemy has been waged with great activity and effectiveness represent only a small portion of the country. In some parts there has been a marked inactivity—officers who are neglecting their duty must get on or get out.'

In the spring of 1920 the I.R.A. was far from being as dangerous as it seemed to the Castle and the Viceregal Lodge. Many Volunteers were very nervous, even in the presence of unarmed civilians. They often prefaced their raids with apologies, and one agreeable young Mayo gunman observed lugubriously, while holding a gun to an old lady's head: 'These are terrible times we live in my lady.'

The majority of the Irish people wanted peace, and at any time in the first part of the year would have agreed with the Bishop of Ross, who described the killing of four policemen by the I.R.A. at Timoleague as 'a callous and deliberate murder'. The Lord Mayor of Dublin, Larry O'Neill, discussed the possibility of a truce with both the Viceroy and General Macready. He thought that the Sinn Fein leaders could arrange a lull in the I.R.A. campaign of assassinations and arson if the military and police stopped raiding for suspected persons. But violence has its own momentum. The attacks on the R.I.C. and their barracks and raids by the Crown Forces continued, and Macready told the Cabinet that he must have another eight battalions. The forces under his command, though imposing on paper, were all under strength and some of the officers and most of the men were inexperienced.

In London the Cabinet was not allowed to forget Ireland even for a day. A hundred and thirty Irish prisoners started another hunger strike at Wormwood Scrubs. Seven thousand Irish demonstrators marched to the prison with a pipe band, and assailed it with shouts of 'Up the Rebels' and 'Up Sinn Fein' and with songs such as 'The Wearing of the Green' and other nationalist ditties. The prisoners smashed the windows and joined in through newspaper megaphones, while the London police protected the Irish demonstrators from being attacked with sticks and stones by anti-Irish demonstrators. Forty-eight thousand dockers in Liverpool threatened to strike in sympathy with the Wormwood Scrubs prisoners, and Thomas Johnson assured the Scottish T.U.C. Conference that 'the only alternative to absolute self-determination in Ireland is the extermination of its people'. The hunger strikers were released in batches.

At Westminster, Asquith argued powerfully against the Government for the immediate offer of Dominion status to Ireland, with county option for Ulster, and Bonar Law unguardedly admitted, in the course of debate, that the real purpose of the Home Rule Bill was to impress foreigners. He was becoming increasingly anxious about Ireland. A Unionist deputation from the South and West of Ireland told him that Waterford had come under the control of a Soviet commissar and three associates. Anything seemed possible in that troubled land, and some business establishments had, in fact, been taken over by workers' committees. Sir Henry Wilson assured Bonar Law that 'he had not begun his Irish troubles yet', and wrote in his diary on the 11th May: 'The Frocks are frightened. Winston suggested that a special force of eight thousand old soldiers be raised at once to reinforce the R.I.C. This, in principle, was also agreed to. . . .As usual I found the Cabinet hopeless. They are terrified about Ireland and, having lost all sense of proportion, thought only of that danger, and completely forget England, Egypt, India, etc., in all of which we are going to have trouble, and serious trouble.' This proposal led to the formation later in the year of the Auxiliary Division of the Royal Irish Constabulary, but its strength never exceeded one thousand five hundred. Sir Henry Wilson's own simple solution to the Irish trouble was to shoot Sinn Feiners by roster if the attacks on the police continued.

Sir Hamar Greenwood went to Dublin to take up his duties as Chief Secretary to Ireland. 'I go to Ireland as a friend of Ireland,' he said. 'I will do my best to bring peace.' Sir Warren Fisher, Permanent Secretary to the Treasury, Mr. A. W. Cope, Second Secretary to the Ministry of Pensions, a director of John Barker, the London department store, and another civil servant went over with him to examine and report on the administration of Dublin Castle. As the result of their recommendations, Sir John Anderson, the Chairman of the Board of Inland Revenue, was appointed Joint Under-Secretary with James Macmahon, who was kept on, it was thought, as a concession to the Roman Catholic Hierarchy.

Sir John Anderson was at the beginning of a remarkable career in the maintenance of law and order and one of increasing responsibility which was to take him to the Permanent Under-Secretaryship at the Home Office during the troubled times of the hunger marches, the means test and the depression; to the Governorship of rebellious Bengal in 1933; to high office at home as Lord Privy Seal and Home Secretary during the war when he gave his name to the domestic bomb shelter; and finally as Chancellor of the Exchequer before he became Lord Waverley and

Chairman of the Port of London Authority. In 1920 he did not seem likely to set the Liffey on fire, or to contain the flood of rebellion. Nor did A. W. Cope, the ex-Customs and Excise detective who succeeded Sir John Taylor as Assistant Secretary. But this man was to play an important part in the events of the next fourteen months. He had a more eventful background than most civil servants. In his day he had been the terror both of West End drinking clubs, which he entered in the character of a *bon viveur* in evening dress, and of East End dives, which he investigated disguised as a docker. His adventures included a knife fight with smugglers in Cornwall, the pursuit of poteen distillers in Ireland, and a bout of fisticuffs with a gigantic Jewess in Poplar. 'The only woman,' he said, 'whom I had to hit as hard as if she were a man.' This pair of very different civil servants began to re-animate the moribund Castle Administration with the help of a number of civil servants sent over from London. At the same time, General Tudor, an officer who had fought with distinction in the Boer War and the Great War, was appointed as Police Adviser to the Viceroy and was put in command of both police forces—the Royal Irish Constabulary and the Dublin Metropolitan Police, and also of the Intelligence and Secret Service. The conduct of affairs was largely taken out of the hands of the Anglo-Irish bureaucracy who had, hitherto, been kings of the Castle, although the ultimate responsibility had lain elsewhere. They thought of Ireland as their native country, even though they considered themselves superior to the 'bog Irish', the gombeen men and saloon-keepers. The newcomers to the Castle suffered from none of the prejudices or inhibitions of the native-born administrator. Like the Black and Tans, they had come to Ireland to do a job, and when it was finished they would leave. The job was twofold: to wear down the Republicans by a campaign of attrition and to find someone with whom to negotiate.

[46]

In the early summer there were, unfortunately, more signs of opposition than of any desire to negotiate. Angier Street in Dublin, for example, had become known to British troops as the 'Dardanelles', so often did the shawly girls hand guns to Volunteers to shoot at soldiers or policemen, and bombs descend from upstairs windows or passing lorries. Down at the docks, on the 20th May, the men refused to unload a ship bringing munitions for the British forces. They were following, in reverse, the example of the London dockers who had refused to load the *Jolly George* with arms for Poland against Soviet Russia. This movement spread to dockers at Dun Laoghaire, where a ship had to be discharged by soldiers. The Irish members of the National Union of Railwaymen then refused to move the train for three days until their representatives had been allowed to inspect it, and see that it carried nothing more lethal than bully beef. They, also, were extending to their own country the principle of a resolution by their own Executive in London which instructed its members not to handle any material intended to help Poland in its war against Russia. At North Wall Dock, a few days later, over four hundred railwaymen were dismissed for refusing to unload arms. This was the beginning of seven months of passive resistance to British military power by Irish transport workers.

The material results of active resistance at the end of May were: three hundred and fifty-one evacuated barracks destroyed and a hundred and five damaged; fifteen occupied barracks destroyed and twenty-five damaged. The I.R.A. had also raided nineteen Coastguard stations and lighthouses for explosives and signalling equipment. They had killed sixty-six policemen and wounded seventy-nine, killed five soldiers and wounded two, and had murdered an unknown number of their own compatriots as suspected spies and traitors. They were galloping, with Gadarene alacrity, into moral degradation and the murky territory

[47]

where the gun is the only lawgiver. The beautiful, the legendary and symbolic Kathleen ni Houlihan was a melancholy and degenerated old trollop by the time they had finished. Over a thousand Black and Tans were distributed over the island to strengthen police posts, while others were on their way, to make, in the words of the *Dublin Police Journal*, 'Ireland hell for rebels to live in'. In London, Sir Hamar Greenwood outlined the policy of which they were the instrument in an interview with the *Chicago Tribune*. 'We won't stand for independence. We won't have a republic. Short of that, if this campaign of violence and anarchy ceases, the Irish people can have any measure of home rule they can agree on.'

10. The ever optimistic Sir Hamar Greenwood, Chief Secretary for Ireland, and the shrewd Joint Under-secretary, Sir John Anderson, leave No. 10 Downing Street after the Cabinet had decided to reinforce Ireland.

11. Professional Soldiers: Field-Marshal Lord French, the Viceroy, and General Macready, the Commander-in-Chief in Ireland.

12. The 'Gun Men': Michael Collins, Director of Intelligence, and Richard Mulcahy, Chief of Staff of the Irish Republican Army, after the Treaty.

13. Soldiers demonstrate their vigilance against ambushers for the benefit of a press photographer. The two men in dark uniforms and peaked caps are Black and Tan reinforcements for an R.I.C. police barracks.

14. Troops, tanks and armoured cars guarded the entrance to Mountjoy Gaol where eighty political prisoners were on hunger strike in April, 1920. Their plight united Irishmen against the Government.

CHAPTER FOUR

The Gunman's Republic

THE MAN who started, and largely directed, the I.R.A.'s campaign against the British Forces was Michael Collins. He was its Adjutant-General, Director of Organisation, Director of Intelligence and, as Minister of Finance in the Dáil, its Paymaster as well. He was a real Irishman, unlike many, if not most of the leaders in Ireland's long story of rebellion, who suffered, in a nationalist sense, from being wholly or partly English. He had, therefore, no disposition to be more Irish than the Irish as had the Englishman, Erskine Childers, a most capable propagandist, whom he suspected of being an agent provocateur. Neither was he less Irish than the Irish, like the half-Yorkshireman Cathal Brugha, the Minister of Defence and founder and director of a firm of ecclesiastical candle-makers, who hated him, and the half-Spaniard, de Valera, with whom he was out of sympathy.

He was born in Cork in 1890. His father was a bachelor until he was sixty-three, when he married a woman forty years his junior—a late marriage even by Irish standards. Michael Collins came to London with a clerkship in the Post Office at £70 a year when he was sixteen. Later he worked in a bank, then in a stockbroker's office in the City. In 1909 he joined the Irish Republican Brotherhood, the secret society which aimed to establish an Irish Republic by force of arms. It became the chief interest of his life. In 1915, fearing that he might be called up, he told his employers that he was going to enlist, received a gratuity for his patriotic spirit, and went back to Ireland. He played a minor but brave part in the 1916 rebellion, and was among those who were interned in England and released in 1917. Later that year he was arrested for making a seditious speech at Longford. It was Sinn Fein's policy to deny the jurisdiction of the courts to the extent of refusing bail. Collins, more sensibly, accepted bail, but did not answer to it, and thus became a wanted man 'on the run'.

He helped to reorganise the Irish Republican Brotherhood and, when most of the leaders of Sinn Fein were arrested in 1918, began his campaign of assassination. The Irish people did not want it and the Church condemned it. The cult of violence demoralised a generation of young Irishmen, as the squalid brutalities of the Civil War showed later. It justified Orange suspicions of the South, and strengthened the hands of those Conservatives at Westminster who were opposed to granting any concessions to Ireland.

In 1920 Michael Collins occupied the place in British demonology that was later taken by men like Menahen Begin of the Palestinian Irgun and Colonel Grivas of the Cypriot Eoka who led similar movements. The so called glorious struggle for liberty which he had started was, paradoxically, only saved from defeat, in the end, by the revulsion of British public opinion against the activities of the Black and Tans who were crushing it.

Michael Collins was a man of irresistible charm for those who succumbed to it, and he behaved overbearingly and with truculence to those who did not. He showed great courage and had remarkable powers of organisation. He preferred 'clever cowards to brave fools'. His intelligence network included agents in the Castle, in the police, the docks, railways, post office, as well as listening posts in the public houses of Dublin. Many Irishmen 'on the run' owed their liberty to a hastily scribbled message: 'There is a warrant out for you. You know what to do. M.C.' His murders were well planned and expertly executed by his

'Squad' with their trusty Parabellum automatics. As a wanted man he raised £375,000 for the Dáil Loan—much of it from unwilling Unionists as the price of safety. The bulk of the fund was lodged in Irish banks in the name of trustees. £25,000 of it was in gold, packed in four boxes weighing about two hundredweight each, and a baby's coffin which were hidden under the concrete floor of a house in Brendan Road in Dublin.

In 1920 he cycled every day from his Ministry of Finance offices in Mary Street and St. Andrew's Street to his Intelligence Office at No. 5 Mespil Road, where he sat working behind lace curtains, a revolver on his desk. He had a price on his head and, more often than not as he cycled openly about Dublin, secret papers hidden in his socks. His narrow escapes made him a legendary figure, a cross between Robin Hood and the Scarlet Pimpernel. 'I do not allow myself to feel that I am on the run,' he said. 'That is my safeguard and prevents me from acting in a manner likely to arouse suspicion.' In a raid on the Sinn Fein Headquarters in Harcourt Street at the beginning of 1920 he bluffed the first policeman who came into the room, walked past as though he were only an unimportant clerk, and ran upstairs to escape through a skylight. But his papers were captured. He had a fastidious mania for documentation; it seemed that his training as a filing clerk in the City would not allow him to destroy any papers. Later a cache of documents which were of no use to him disclosed the names of all but one of his agents in the Castle

It seems astonishing that he was never caught. Agents, sent to find him, had no difficulty in meeting him. There was Quinlisk, the broken-down ex-prisoner-of-war, who had joined Casement's Brigade in Germany in 1916. He tried, very ineptly, to betray Collins who had gone out of his way to help him, and was shot for his pains in Cork. Fergus Brian Mulloy, a soldier with an English accent who professed to be a patriotic Irishman, was taken straight to

Collins when he promised to provide arms, but fared no better. The British Secret Serviceman, Byrne, who had made a reputation for himself as a Labour agitator in England under the name of Jameson, came nearest to catching him. He represented himself as a Bolshevik agent able to smuggle arms, and even handed over a few revolvers to show his good faith. One of Collins' agents in the Castle got wind of his plan to capture Collins, and Byrne came under suspicion. At their next meeting Collins, with deliberate carelessness, allowed him to overlook part of a fake document which referred to a cache of important papers at No. 9 Iona Drive. The police ransacked the house, while the owner, a Loyalist ex-Lord Mayor of Dublin, stood by in his night clothes protesting: 'You are raiding your friends. Do you know I received the King? I had twenty minutes' conversation with him.' This genial practical joke provided another job for the 'Squad'. Byrne was found shot dead in Ballymun Road on the 2nd March. The revelation of his real activities caused anger and alarm in Labour circles in England.

Such cloak-and-dagger exploits and the glamour attaching to Michael Collins' name disguised the nature of a movement which quickly lost any constructive purpose it may have had. The Dáil did not accept responsibility for the activities of the I.R.A. until March, 1921, by which time the public conscience had been deadened by the forces of violence on both sides. In the summer of 1920, the Dáil still adhered to Sinn Fein's peaceful programme of establishing itself as the *de facto* government and of securing international recognition as an independent republic. The elections of County Council, Rural District Councils and Boards of Poor Law Guardians in June gave Sinn Fein an overwhelming majority. The Local Government Board of the Dáil circulated all County Councils, urging them to pass resolutions of loyalty to the Dáil. They all obliged, either out of conviction or because of intimidation, though some later recanted. The Dáil Arbitration Courts, set up by a decree, were functioning in twenty-eight of Ireland's thirty-two counties. Any litigant who went to the Government's courts of law did so in peril of his life. The Republican courts arbitrated with fairness according to a code drawn up in June, 1920, by, among others, Mr. Hector Hughes, later a K.C. and the Labour Member of Parliament for Aberdeen. Unionists took their cases to these courts, and barristers and solicitors pleaded their cases at their sittings, although anyone taking part in these proceedings was technically guilty of an offence under the Crimes Act of 1887.

The spectacle of a plaintiff owing allegiance to one government suing a defendant who supported another in the courts of a self-styled Republic which was an illegal organisation was diverting, but it did not entirely conceal the uglier side of Republican justice. The courts also professed to try persons suspected of being spies or traitors. The accused was usually not present at the tribunals, which followed no recognised rules of evidence, with the result that rumour and malice delivered many innocent landowners, farm workers, ex-soldiers and policemen to execution by the gunmen. At the end of June the Dáil also created Land Courts which considered and settled about three hundred cases. Many Unionist landowners were anxious to dispose of their property at almost any cost, but they were awarded fair prices.

English and foreign journalists who attended these arbitration courts were impressed by the justice dispensed, and were led, with less reason, to report that Sinn Fein with its police, its courts, its army and local authorities was the ruler of Ireland. The correspondent of *The Daily News* even reported that 'Ireland is taking pleasure in law and order for the first time within the memory of man'. The facts hardly supported this conclusion. In many parts of the country only the presence of British troops prevented land-grabbing and cattle-driving from degenerating into rural anarchy. The execution of supposed spies and traitors was almost a daily occurrence. The I.R.A. had killed three more policemen in ambushes and wounded thirteen in the month of June. A taste for arson, notoriously an appetite which grows, extended from empty barracks to coastguard stations on which the safety of shipping depended. The Dáil was not in control of the gunmen: 'Our war policy was not popular,' Dan Breen, one of the most eminent of them has recorded. 'The military authorities did not seem to want it. The political wing certainly did not.' The gunmen had taken over the conduct of affairs, and had begun to impose their standard of values on the youth of Ireland. Children's street games were all ambushes, and a popular infant pastime was to re-enact the murder of Alan Bell.

The main function of the banned Ministries of the Dáil was to show Irishmen that they could govern themselves and to persuade the rest of the world that the Dáil was the government of Ireland. A' commission of Enquiry into Irish Industrial Resources produced some over-sanguine reports of an independent Ireland's economic prospects. A Co-operative Fishery Society existed in name alone. A Department of Gaelic published half a dozen text-books, and the Department of Agriculture planted a few thousand trees. The Ministry of Labour enjoyed a certain *réclame* because of the character of the Minister, Countess Markievicz. This Anglo-Irish lady had been born as Constance Gore-Booth in Carlton House Terrace in 1868. She was a debutante of the year 1888, and an intrepid rider to hounds before she became embroiled in nationalist and revolutionary politics. She founded the *Fianna*, the Irish Boy Scouts movement, and as early as 1909 was training them in the use of arms. She fought in the 1916 rebellion and was sentenced to death for taking a pot-shot, which missed, at a doctor standing in the window of the Unionist Club. Her sentence was commuted to penal servitude for life and she was released with the other prisoners of the Easter Rising in 1917.

This already legendary woman lent a romantic gloss to accounts of the Dáil in the foreign Press, even though she could not increase its effectiveness. Her errant Polish husband, Count Casimir, treated Ireland and its politics as a joke. There was, indeed, a farcical undertone to this struggle in spite of the many terrible things that were done on both sides. Racing went on uninterrupted even in the most savage phases; gunmen on the run, soldiers and Black and Tans, priests and Orangemen enjoyed the sport together without disturbance. General Macready had let it be known that if any members of the Crown Forces were molested on the course he would close down racing tracks all over Ireland. Hostilities ceased for Dublin Horse Show week. It was possible for Anglo-Irish civil servants to find out, by discreet enquiry, whether they were on the list for assassination, and therefore have to remain immured in the Castle, or whether they could live safely at home.

While the members of the Dáil were on the run, nearly every important official connected with the Dublin Castle Administration was virtually interned in the Castle, sometimes with his wife and family. They lived in overcrowded conditions, often three to a room, sometimes two to a bed. One official sallied out for a time, under heavy escort, to lunch at his club, but his fellow members, fearing that he was compromising them, urged him to stay in the Castle. A dancing class once a week, an occasional game of tennis on hard courts laid-out inside the Castle precincts, the chance of an assignation with one of the pretty secretaries who were being recruited as typists for the Intelligence Section could help to lighten, but not dispel, an oppressive claustrophobia.

Conditions for the soldiers and police in their barracks were not much better. There was little action, but there was no lull in an atmosphere of suspense. Any road might lead to an ambush; the most harmless-looking civilian might suddenly draw a gun and fire. The urge, after an attack, to hit back at anyone within range was strong. The Black and Tans had already begun to show that they could not resist the temptation. Some of them, stationed in dull and desolate Irish towns and villages, found, like many of the male inhabitants, that there was nothing much to do but drink. Irishmen in many parts of the South and West had become unpleasantly used to rough handling by half-drunk and abusive Black and Tans and many publicans had the unhappy experience of supplying them with free drink at the pistol point. In May there had been cases of wild shooting in Limerick and the bombing and burning of houses in Thurles and Bantry as reprisals for attempts on police or barracks.

General Tudor, the new police chief, rearmed the R.I.C. with rifles and machine guns, fortified barracks with steel shutters and provided new transport. In June, lorry loads of Black and Tans moved into the offensive. They tore down village streets firing their rifles at random to the peril of anyone who happened to be in the way, often singing incongruously:

> We are the boys of the R.I.C.
> As happy as happy can be.

Even such modified forms of Black and Tannery rightly caused dismay in England where policemen did not behave in like manner, and where the majority of the Press, from *The Times* to the *Daily Herald*, had already aligned itself against the Government's handling of Ireland. A further shock was administered to British public opinion by a mutiny of the R.I.C. at Listowel on the 17th June. They refused to hand over their barracks to the military and be posted to outlying barracks in the dangerous countryside General Tudor and Lt.-Col. Smyth, D.S.O., a one-armed veteran of the Great War who had been appointed Divisional Commissioner of the R.I.C. for Munster, went to investigate. The Colonel addressed the assembled constables. The words he was supposed to have used were fully reported in the British Press and were the subject of angry questions and accusations in the House of Commons: 'Well, men, I have something of interest to tell you: something I'm sure you would not want your wives to hear,' Colonel Smyth was represented as having said. '. . . .Now, men, Sinn Fein has had all the sport up to the present, and we are going to have the sport now. The police are not in sufficient strength to do anything but hold their barracks. This is not enough, for as long as we remain on the defensive, so long will Sinn Fein have the whip hand. We must take the offensive, and beat Sinn Fein with its own tactics. . . .

'. . . .If a police barracks is burned or if the barracks already occupied is not suitable, then the best house in the locality is to be commandeered, the occupants thrown into the gutter. Let them die there—the more the merrier. Police and military will patrol the country at least five nights a week. They are not to confine themselves to the main roads, but make across the country, lie in ambush and, when civilians are seen approaching, shout "Hands up!" Should the order be not immediately obeyed, shoot and shoot with effect. If the persons approaching carry their hands in their pockets, or are in any way suspicious-looking, shoot them down.

'You may make mistakes occasionally and innocent persons may be shot, but that cannot be helped, and you are bound to get the right parties some time. The more you shoot, the better I will like you, and I assure you no policeman will get into trouble for shooting any man. . . .' Five constables resigned at the end of this address—one of them later entered the Church, to become a Colonial bishop before his death.

The medium by which this speech reached the outside world was *The Irish Bulletin*, a skilfully edited propaganda sheet which was circulated to the foreign Press from Dublin. It is unlikely that the report was based on a short-hand note by a constable, and Sir John Anderson, in Dublin Castle, said that it was inconceivable that Smyth could have made this statement. Colonel Smyth gave his own version two days later, but even that exhorted the police to shoot first, even if mistakes were made. Whatever his exact words were, the subsequent behaviour of the police largely corroborated the original report.

Soldiers showed that they also could break out. On the 26th June Brigadier Lucas and two other officers took a few days' leave to go fishing near Fermoy. Up to then no attacks had been made on officers engaged in sport, and it was assumed that there was a tacit agreement to consider it a neutral activity, like horse racing. It was well known, for example, that such a natural target for gunmen as Mr. Wylie, the Law Adviser at Dublin Castle, regularly turned out with the Meath Hounds without mishap. But these officers did not take into account the military resource of the redoubtable Commander Liam Lynch, the man who had disarmed the Church parade at Fermoy in September, 1919. They found him and a group of Volunteers waiting for them when they returned to their cottage after fishing in the evening. They were kidnapped and spirited away in motor cars. The next evening the troops at Fermoy smashed windows, killed one man and caused £18,000 damage with rifle fire and grenades, in what their Brigade Commander later called 'an over-zealous display of loyalty'.

This incident illustrates the British Government's in-decisive approach to the Irish problem. General Macready discovered from the Intelligence Service that the kidnapping of the officers had been inspired by local initiative and not ordered by I.R.A. Headquarters. He proposed to Sir Hamar Greenwood that six members of the I.R.A. in Cork should be arrested as hostages for the safety of the Brigade Com-mander, but Sir Hamar and Sir John Anderson demurred on the grounds that there would be no evidence to implicate the hostages, and also that they might go on hunger strike. Then, although Brigadier Lucas wrote a letter asking that no effort should be made to trace him, with the implication that his life would be endangered by such an attempt, the Government ordered an organised drive to be made with troops and aeroplanes to find him.

While this hopeless operation was in progress, General Macready had to defend the Brigadier against the wrath of Winston Churchill, the Secretary of State for War, by 'pointing out' as he wrote, 'that though it was certainly thoughtless on the part of the officer to endeavour to while away the monotony of existence by indulging in sport, it had to be remembered that under the situation as it existed no official, civil or military, was exempted from the same fate, nor would they be until such time as the Government chose to recognise that the country was in a state of war.'

Lloyd George was not prepared to recognise this. He was looking over his shoulder at the United States, and was afraid of offending world Catholic opinion but for which Ireland, he said, 'should be made mince meat of by the military'. He announced instead that he was prepared to discuss Ireland with Sinn Fein or anyone else who had authority to speak for Ireland. Arthur Griffith replied with a statement that 'representatives of Ireland are prepared to meet accredited representatives of Britain'. But as Sinn Fein was committed to an Independent Republic and Lloyd George insisted that Ireland should remain within the Empire, and Ulster should not be coerced, there was still no common ground on which to meet.

Nevertheless, the Government was being assailed by an increasingly vocal opposition. On the left the Miners' Federation, which was threatening trouble on its own account at home, passed a resolution demanding the withdrawal of British troops from Ireland. On the right, Lord

Henry Cavendish-Bentinck formed the 'Peace with Ireland Council'. The secretary was a promising young Conservative, Sir Oswald Mosley, later a promising young figure in the Labour Government, and finally, best known perhaps, as the founder and leader of the British Union of Fascists. A committee of English Catholics was formed to oppose the Government's policy, and the editor of *The Catholic Herald* had already been sent to prison earlier in the year for sedition. G. K. Chesterton, Hilaire Belloc and Bernard Shaw denounced the oppression of Ireland on platforms and in print. Horatio Bottomley, Liberal M.P. and well-known patriot and swindler, also found Ireland an excellent theme for his demagogic brand of oratory and a suitable subject for his magazine *John Bull*, which he used to promote his frauds. He went to prison in 1922. At this time the attack on the Government made up with variety what it lacked in force.

Brigadier Lucas, who was well treated by his captors, eventually escaped to solve one of General Macready's problems, but did not materially improve the anomalous position in which he found himself. The I.R.A. was at war with his forces, but the British Army was not at war with the I.R.A. It was still officially limited to helping the civil power maintain order, and not only in the South of Ireland. In the last week of June, Protestant mobs in Derry in the North started an anti-Catholic riot, shooting, burning and looting. Twenty civilians had been killed by the time police and troops arrived in sufficient strength to restore order. Another such outbreak in Belfast was quelled before any great damage was done. Meanwhile, railwaymen in the South were bringing the railway system to a standstill, and tying up troops and transport on supply duties, by refusing to carry any war stores, or work any train carrying armed soldiers or police. Several hundred railwaymen had been dismissed, but there was no sign of their giving way. The Executive of the National Union of Railwaymen in London passed strong resolutions in their support, but gave them no help beyond sending a deputation to the Prime Minister who insisted that the Government had 'really got to be absolutely adamant'. The general secretary of the N.U.R., J. H. Thomas, publicly displayed for the first time his undoubted talent for saying one thing and doing another. Irish trade unionists were not impressed by him, and were less surprised than their brothers across the sea when his political career finally ended in disgrace. As a Cabinet Minister he unwisely gave a hint to a racing friend of one of the provisions of the Budget in 1936, which enabled some gentlemen in the City to do very well for themselves and caused a scandal and a public enquiry. He resigned his office and his seat in the House in floods of tears, and was even refused his pension by the union which he had served well by his own, sometimes dubious, lights, although he paraded his family on the platform to excite pity.

In one way and another, British policy had once more begun to unite Irishmen everywhere. On the 28th June, three hundred and fifty men of the Connaught Rangers stationed at Jullindur, in the Punjab, laid down their arms and refused 'to soldier for England' any longer as a protest at the news from Ireland. Sixty-two were court martialed, one executed, and others sentenced to terms of penal servitude for periods of two to twenty years. They were released a year later. In Dublin the Unionist Chamber of Commerce was so alarmed by the growing disorder that it threw its Unionism overboard and proposed that the Government should immediately concede a measure of self-government to Ireland, subject to Lloyd George's provisos. In London, opposition to the Government was growing from day to day, and even so staunch a Conservative as Lord Robert Cecil, later Viscount Chelwood, had declared: 'We are drifting through anarchy and humiliation to an Irish Republic. We will never settle the Irish question except in accordance with the wishes of the Irish people.' Surveying the melancholy course of events from a different point of view, Sir Henry Wilson wrote in his diary on the 28th June: 'I am very unhappy about Ireland. I don't see any determination or driving power in the Cabinet and I really believe we shall be kicked out.'

CHAPTER FIVE

The Gathering Storm

THE STATE of the country in July, 1920, was not bad enough to prevent English visitors from spending their holidays in Ireland. In at least a dozen of the twenty-six southern counties not a shot was fired during the entire month. There were, in all, about fifty I.R.A. attacks and ambushes against Coastguard Stations, police barracks and transport. Very few attacks were pressed home against resistance, and when they were, a number of Volunteers 'went to America'—the I.R.A.'s euphemism for being killed in action.

These disorders stood out starkly because they occurred in a predominantly civilian context. Many more British soldiers were being killed in Mesopotamia, where the Shiah tribesmen were resisting inclusion in the newly-created British Mandate of Iraq, without making news, or exciting any interest at all except for their nearest and dearest. Nevertheless, the façade of everyday life was being severely dented. There were soldiers to be seen everywhere, and they made a great show of force, even if it were not being used in a war-like sense. An Irishman in Dublin or Cork might find himself stopped and searched by different bodies of soldiers or police as many as half a dozen times a day. A farmer, hearing a knock on his door at night and the command to open up, would not know whether to expect a military search party, Black and Tans, an I.R.A. gunman on the run, or a posse of ordinary robbers of whom there were a growing number. By the ordinary peacetime standards of citizens in London or Birmingham, conditions

[63]

in Ireland were appalling. As an old Dublin woman was heard to observe: 'Mary and the Saints protect us. It do be terrible the times we are living in now. What with them Blacksies and them Tansies, the Military and the I.R.A., we poor women never know from one moment to another when we wouldn't be hurled into maternity.'

Cork was the chief centre of disorder. In July, Volunteers made four attacks on Coastguard stations, ambushed a stores lorry, killing one officer and wounding three soldiers, and in a number of other attacks, most of which misfired, killed one more constable and wounded another. Casualties would have been higher had the marksmanship been better. The Volunteers were surer shots at point-blank range. At 10.30 p.m. on the 17th July, Volunteers entered the County Club in Cork, where Colonel Smyth of the R.I.C. was taking a drink with County Inspector Craig. Three of the Volunteers guarded the entrance and the others went upstairs. One walked up to him and said, according to the legend: 'Were not your orders to shoot at sight? Well you are in sight now, so prepare.' Whether this improbable speech was made or not, the Colonel was shot dead and the County Inspector wounded. The assailants ran out into the street to mingle with the crowds coming out of cinemas. On the next day General Strickland, the Commander of the British forces in the area, ordered a curfew between 10 p.m. and 3 a.m. Armoured cars and parties of military and police patrolled the streets. Another attack was made on a Black and Tan patrol in the evening. It was a Sunday, at a time when the streets were crowded with family parties returning from the seaside and country. In the shooting affray that followed one civilian was killed and half a dozen wounded. The citizens of Cork went to bed to the sound of exploding bombs and rifle fire, the rattle of armoured cars and the yells of trigger-happy Black and Tans in their Crossley tenders. But in this strange war the ladies of Cork still assembled as usual next morning in the cafés of Patrick

15. Countess Constance Markievicz, the Dail's Minister of Labour, with Cathal O'Shannon of the Irish Trades Union Congress and Labour Party. She fought in 1916, was condemned to death and reprieved. He was one of the Irish delegates at the international socialist congresses at Berne and Amsterdam in 1919.

16. A great Irishman, but no Sinn Feiner: Field-Marshal Sir Henry Wilson, the Chief of Imperial General Staff. He held politicians, whom he called 'the Frocks', in utter contempt—particularly Lloyd George.

Street to discuss the excitements of the previous night over their coffee and cakes. Even in the areas where the fighting was fiercest, life went on very much as usual, although all meetings and assemblies were prohibited in the curfew area and the nationalist magistrates of the City and County resigned their British commissions with suspicious unanimity. Some, perhaps, were actuated by the same motive that induced the Unionists to subscribe to the Dáil Loan. The gunman could be powerfully persuasive. One of them at least caused a revulsion of feeling even among Sinn Feiners by shooting an R.I.C. sergeant in the porch of Bandon Church as he was coming out after Mass. The Bishop of Cork inflicted on the man who shot the sergeant, 'or the abettors by command, council or otherwise, the canonical punishment called Interdict'. A British soldier was also assassinated in Bandon, and two I.R.A. commandants, Hales and Harte, were captured and tortured as a reprisal, not by Black and Tans, but by two Irish officers serving in the Essex Regiment. This case was not exceptional: many of the other atrocities attributed at the time to the Black and Tans were committed by the regular members of the Royal Irish Constabulary who hated Sinn Fein and the I.R.A. far more than did the British ex-serviceman, who had no interest in Irish politics. Hales managed to smuggle a message out of prison to Michael Collins describing his ill-treatment. Collins wrote to Arthur Griffith:

'. . . It is important, in my opinion, that a really good case should be made of this statement; that it should be forwarded to Séan T., for instance, to present it to the French Department; that it should be given out to journalists everywhere here and on the Continent. It should then be taken point by point in the Propaganda Department, and rubbed in from day to day. Particularly the treatment meted out by us to Brigadier General Lucas should be contrasted with the treatment meted out by them to Brigadier General Hales.'

Irish propaganda was efficiently organised, and Hales' statement appeared in both *The Manchester Guardian* and *The Daily News*, to administer another shock to an increasingly anxious British public.

On the 19th July two constables were killed in an ambush near Tuam, in Galway. On the next evening Black and Tans ran amok. They raided public houses, looted the contents and set fire to the town hall and a number of shops. The Bishop of Galway wrote to General Macready, demanding an enquiry. The R.I.C. had suffered losses in Limerick, and the nerves of the Black and Tans, who were the main targets, were on edge with the constant sniping. They beat up members of the Confraternity of the Holy Faith as they returned from a meeting, shot up the village of Bruff, killing one man and a boy as a reprisal; they broke windows and burned houses in Kilmallock. The fire-brigades of Ireland were fully occupied. British officers, noticing that any building they surveyed as possible billets was immediately set on fire, made a point of ostentatiously examining Sinn Fein halls in towns and villages, thereby neatly turning the fire raisers against their own side.

In Tipperary the Volunteers were hanging back. A letter from the Commander of the Third Tipperary Brigade to the Chief of Staff complained of desertions, neglect of duty and cowardice, and advocated executions as a means 'of making the terror behind greater than the terror in front'. One attack was made on an R.I.C. barracks, but the constables held it with the loss of one man, although it was set on fire. Two R.I.C. men were wounded in an ambush near Upperchurch and Black and Tans burned a creamery and private houses in the town as a reprisal. A Tipperary gunman also shot the caretaker of a Unionist landlord. Kerry Volunteers were more active: they attacked two

R.I.C. barracks, but without success, and killed three constables in ambushes, wounding thirteen others. In Dublin, Volunteers raided the unguarded General Post Office and removed military mail. The Viceroy, at the Viceregal Lodge, received his post stamped 'Censored by the I.R.A.' They surprised an armed guard at Kingsbridge Station, seized arms and set three railway wagons on fire, and on two or three other occasions they disarmed police or military. They wounded a soldier in Westmoreland Street and, on the 30th July, three men, presumably Volunteers, walked into the office of the Rt. Honourable Frank Brooke at Westland Row Station and shot him dead. He was Chairman of the Dublin and South East Railways, an Irish Privy Councillor and a friend of the Viceroy. Volunteers in all districts also prevented Irishmen and women from emigrating, both by threats and force, in accordance with a Manifesto from the Ministry of Defence which began:

'The enemy has declared that there are too many young men in Ireland, and he is anxious to clear them out. It suited his purpose to refuse them passports during the war, but he will now give them every facility to emigrate. These facilities must not be availed of. Ireland wants all her young men. Their presence in the country is more necessary now than ever. It is because of their growing numbers and their efficient military organisation that the British Army of Occupation is in its present state of disorganisation. The long-drawn-out struggle has reached its final stages, and Ireland is winning. No one realises this more clearly than the enemy. His recent admissions prove it. His cunning and brute force have availed him nothing in the end. There is just one chance left for him, that is, to stimulate emigration.' This nonsense meant that peace-loving Irish people who did not like the I.R.A. campaign and had somewhere better to go, had to stay and lump it.

The scale of I.R.A. activities was not impressive, but

[67]

men who had fought in the Great War found that they imposed a greater strain than service in France. Soldiers under stricter discipline than the Black and Tans were often on the point of taking the law into their own hands, as they had at Fermoy. There were signs that the tension was too much for them. One apparently demented officer with a party of troops burst in on a sitting of the Dáil Commission on Industries at Carrick-on-Shannon, held a drumhead court-martial, sentenced the chairman to death, and had already sent a soldier for a rope before the regular R.I.C. intervened to stop the lunacy.

In London, Sir Henry Wilson became increasingly anxious about the conduct of the Black and Tans, though not on humanitarian grounds. He found that Lloyd George harboured 'an amazing theory that someone was murdering two Sinn Feiners to every loyalist the Sinn Feiners murdered. I told him, of course, that this was absolutely not so but he seemed to be satisfied that a counter-murder association was the best answer to Sinn Fein murders. A crude idea of statemanship, and he will have a rude awakening.' On the 11th July Sir Henry discussed Ireland with Winston Churchill and 'told him that the present policy was suicidal, and that it would lead to our being put out of Ireland, that we must take strong measures or retire, that if we retired we lost our Empire, that before taking strong measure we must convince England that they were necessary. . . .But I did not make much impression.' It was becoming increasingly difficult to convince England that strong measures were necessary.

On the 13th July a Special Trade Union Congress met in London under the chairmanship of J. H. Thomas and, by a narrow majority, passed a resolution demanding a truce, and the establishment of 'an Irish Parliament with full Dominion Powers in all Irish affairs, with adequate protection for minorities'. A proposal that the Irish people should determine their own form of government was heavily defeated. The Congress closed with a resolution condemning the military occupation of Ireland. 'We recommend,' it said, 'a general down-tools policy, and call on all trades unions here represented to carry out this policy, each according to its own constitution, by taking a ballot or otherwise.' This resolution was mere shadow boxing of a type that the British trade unions developed between the wars and perfected at the time of the Spanish Civil War. It was, nonetheless, a threat to the Government.

General Macready was opposed to the imposition of martial law, because he did not consider that he had the military strength to enforce it, or think that the Government would be able to maintain it 'until such time as they had the country behind them in the matter (which, judging by the English Press, was very far from being the case)'. The generals seemed to have had an acuter sense of the effect the Black and Tans were having on British public opinion than the politicians. But in July, 1920, he thought the situation so serious, both in the North and in the South, that he suggested to the Government that martial law might give the army a better chance of dealing with 'the element of disorder', even if it were not entirely effective. The Government decided instead to increase the power of the military by introducing fresh legislation.

In the latter half of July, trouble in Northern Ireland made a more serious call on the services of troops and police than did the sporadic activities of the I.R.A. in the South. After the rioting in Derry, the celebration of the July anniversaries of the Battle of the Boyne in 1690 and the Battle of Aughrim in 1691 seemed likely to lead to serious disorders. These minor engagements in the War of the Grand Alliance, waged by Louis XIV against Great Britain, Holland and Spain, are unknown to many educated Englishmen today, but the memory of them is an essential part of the Orangeman's spiritual equipment. In the first of these battles, William III's army of Dutchmen, Danes and Northern Irishmen defeated the deposed James II's army of Frenchmen and Southern Irishmen who had been led to support the Stuart cause by the Earl of Tyrconnell. In the second, a Dutch general, commanding William of Orange's troops, defeated a French general commanding James II's troops. William III was able to reconquer the island without difficulty, and to establish Protestantism, once and for all time, as the official religion of Great Britain. The Earl of Tyrconnell died of apoplexy.

The anniversary of these events on Orangeman's Day on 12th July was traditionally an occasion for Protestant outrages against Catholics. In 1920 there were 820,000 Protestants in the Six Counties and 430,000 Roman Catholics. In the rest of Ireland there were 2,812,000 Catholics and 327,000 Protestants; Sinn Fein did not preach religious discrimination, though some of its followers practised it; only in the North were religious riots deliberately incited. But in 1920, the momentous day, the 12th July, passed quietly. Troops and police, both Regulars and Black and Tans, were out in force, and leaders of both political parties, the Protestant Unionists and the Catholic Nationalists, used their influence to keep order. Sir Edward Carson, however, the man who, above all others, had criticised the Government for not quelling disorder, made a speech that day which sowed the seeds of a riotous crop of violence only a few days later.

Many people thought, like General Macready, that the I.R.A. campaign in the South was 'due mainly, if not entirely, to the example set by Carson in the North', and the General attributed to him 'a large measure of responsibility for the blood spilt throughout the length and breadth of the island'. Carson was the leader of the Ulster Unionists, whose name expressed their policy. They believed that Ireland was an indivisible part of the United Kingdom. When Asquith's Liberal Government passed the Irish Home Rule Bill in 1912, he had organised rebellion and mutiny in the North, and had forced the Government to capitulate and offer Partition as an alternative policy. With this background, it is difficult to absolve him of the guilt for the events that followed nine days after his address to 120,000 Orangemen during the celebrations of the 12th July. Speaking of Sinn Fein, he said:

'They have all kinds of insidious methods and organisations at work. Sometimes it is the Church. That does not make much way in Ulster. The more insidious method is tacking on the Sinn Fein question and the Irish Republican question to the Labour question. (A voice: "Ireland is the most Labour centre in the United Kingdom.") I know that. What I say is this—these men who come forward posing as friends of Labour care no more about Labour than does the man in the moon. Their real object, and the real insidious nature of their propaganda, is that they may mislead and bring about disunity amongst our own people; and in the end, before we know where we are, we may find ourselves in the same bondage and slavery as is the rest of Ireland in the South and West.

'Beware of these insidious methods. Our duty is an absolutely clear one, and we must state it clearly on a day like this. We have been handed down, from the time of the battle of the Boyne and the siege of Derry—and they may have another siege before long—we have handed down great traditions and great privileges, and in our Orange Order we have undertaken to preserve those and to hand them on to our children, and we must proclaim today clearly that, come what will, and be the consequences what they may, we in Ulster will tolerate no Sinn Fein—(cheers) —no Sinn Fein organisation, no Sinn Fein methods.'

This equation of Sinn Fein, Catholicism and Labour as the triple force threatening Ulster's ancient heritage became the theme of other Orange speakers and of many letters to the Press of Northern Ireland, and it was not long before this propaganda had its effect. At a dinner-hour meeting at the South Yard in Belfast, on the 21st July, the Unionist and Protestant dock workers adopted a resolution which denied the right to work to anyone refusing to sign an undertaking that he was not a member of Sinn Fein, and would not join it. Two hours later Protestant dockworkers, armed with sledge hammers and iron bars, swooped on Catholic workers, beat them up, threw them into the channel and pelted them with rivets. Fighting spread along the waterfront.

The police and troops arrived at the yards to quell this outbreak, but the stone had been flung and the ripples extended far into the city. Wild rumours that many Catholics had been killed brought Nationalists and some Sinn Feiners out on to the streets. By six o'clock fierce fighting had erupted, and the police were unable to separate the Protestant and Catholic crowds who were fighting one another with bricks and stones. The troops were called in at about eight-fifteen. They were stoned and shot at by a Catholic crowd, and returned the fire, killing one man. After an uneasy lull, fighting broke out once more and the military fired again, killing two more Catholics. As night fell, gangs of Orange hooligans smashed the street lamps and fired on police and troops, who once more fired back, killing a woman. During the night Protestant looters made merry and caused considerable damage, particularly to public houses and spirit grocers.

The next day gangs of Unionists toured a number of works to expel 'papists' and 'rotten prods', as Protestants who were not Unionists were known in the Orange vocabulary. Some 'prods' were even rotten enough to be members of Sinn Fein. At night a large crowd of drunken Orangemen attacked the Roman Catholic Church of St. Matthew. They fired on the soldiers and police who were called in to save the church. This time the crowds were so menacing that the troops were ordered to open fire with Lewis guns. Several people were killed. Later the same

night Lewis guns came into action again to disperse crowds
of Catholics and Orangemen who were firing both at one
another and at the troops trying to separate them. Order
seemed to be restored the next day, the 23rd July, until the
evening, when a huge Orange mob stormed a convent in
Newtownards Road, setting it on fire. The sisters had,
fortunately, been taken to safety the previous day. The fire-
brigade extinguished the flames behind a screen of soldiers,
who again had to defend themselves by returning the fire
from the crowd.

Peace returned to Belfast after eighteen people had been
killed and two hundred wounded in three days of rioting.
The pogrom raged for another day in some neighbouring
towns, particularly Banbridge, where Catholics had refused
to close their shops or show any sign of respect to the
funeral cortège of Colonel Smyth who had been murdered
in Cork. In Derry, which had already suffered riots during
the last week of June, a Conciliation Committee, composed
of Protestants and Catholics, prevented another outbreak
of violence. In Belfast, peace patrols of clergymen of all
denominations stopped the sectarian fever from breaking
out again, and the Lord Mayor threatened to take drastic
measures against any disturbers of the peace.

The riots in Belfast were the subject of another angry
Irish debate in the House of Commons in which Joseph
Devlin, the Nationalist member for Belfast, accused Sir
Edward Carson of having provoked them. Sir Edward
defended himself with vigour, if not conviction. 'I deplore
it,' he said. 'I don't want retaliation. But let us be reason-
able.' He reminded the House that Colonel Smyth, a
native of Banbridge, had been murdered and that the
Southern Irish railwaymen had refused to transport his
body. 'Are we the only people who are never to have a
feeling about these matters?' He declared some weeks later
that 'I am prouder of my friends in the shipyards than of
any other friends I have in the whole world'. Sir Hamar

Greenwood did not support his unconvincing justification of the Belfast pogrom, but he had no difficulty in disposing of Devlin's further charge that the police and troops had taken sides.

In Belfast the return of order did not include the return of Catholic workers to their employment. Almost the whole of the Catholic population was out of work. Between Carson's speech on the 12th July and the disturbances, the National Union of Railwaymen had passed a resolution at their Congress in Belfast stating that 'without complete unity amongst the working classes, who should not allow either religious or political differences to prevent their emancipation, which can be achieved through a great international brotherhood the world over, no satisfactory progress can be made'. But such admirable sentiments found little support in Ulster which 'clung like ivy to the vine', in the words of a Unionist pamphlet, 'to the old faith—the Protestant faith—that has made England and Scotland what they are'. On the last day of the month the City Council considered a resolution calling on it to influence employers to do everything possible to restore the right of employment to their Catholic workers. An amendment that this could only be done when the assassins in the South had been brought to justice was carried by thirty-five votes to five. Ulster was set on a course of arson and violence which was even uglier, at times, than the disturbances in the South.

Michael Collins had unwittingly helped these developments. By organising his campaign of assassination in the South, he had played straight into the hands of such enemies of the Republic as Sir Edward Carson, who wanted to divide Ireland, and the Ulster employers, a ruthless body who were, at the same time, glad to encourage and profit by dissensions among their workpeople in the post-war days of threatening class warfare. Dock workers, Protestant and Catholic, who had worked harmoniously together for years, and had stood together in a strike for a forty-four-hour week in February, 1919, were now divided into hostile sections with Protestants driving Catholic members of their own union from work. As a member of the Unionist Council observed: 'The Ulster operative and workers divided are more easily exploited than when they are united.' The I.R.A., with a political outlook that extended no farther than the sights on a gun barrel, next decided to apply a boycott on Ulster goods; Volunteers widened the war of liberation to take in tobacconist shops in the South, where they destroyed stocks of cigarettes manufactured in Northern Ireland. The Dáil was at first opposed to the boycott, as most of its members realised that any form of warfare, whether armed or economic, against the North divided the country in two and denied the principle of a united Ireland. But the gunmen were making the running. The Dáil later ratified the I.R.A. boycott, and enacted a scale of penalties for trades people who stocked Ulster goods. Partition was, thereby, tacitly accepted in the South to the extent that it was not even an issue in the civil war after the Treaty. Sinn Fein, as well as the Unionists, had abandoned a principle.

In England almost the entire Press, with the exception of the ultra-Conservative *Morning Post*, was displaying opposition in varying degrees to the Government's handling of Ireland. *The Manchester Guardian* and *The Daily News* were the most forthright in their condemnations, and *The Westminster Gazette* neatly summed up the course of events in Ireland, and the general reaction to them, when it commented editorially: 'Policemen are shot almost daily and their comrades eventually get out of hand and begin to attack the civilian population. This development means utter bankruptcy of government and must be resisted at all costs.' On the 25th July the Trade Union Congress submitted proposals for Dominion Home Rule to the Prime Minister, who replied: 'I can see no sign that Sinn

Fein is prepared to discuss anything except the thing which is absolutely indiscussible . . . the setting up of an absolutely independent authority.'

The differences between Lloyd George and Sinn Fein seemed unbridgeable, but the gulf between them was no wider than it was a year later at the time of the truce and the beginning of negotiations. Both Mr. Mark Sturgis, Sir John Anderson's private secretary, and Mr. 'Andy' Cope, the Assistant Under-Secretary, were to be seen on the fringes of Sinn Fein society. The clubs and pubs of Dublin and the corridors of Westminster were buzzing with rumours of impending peace at the end of July, but Arthur Griffith announced in a statement to the Press that no approach had been made to Dáil Eireann. There was no talk of peace in the I.R.A. In an article entitled 'Keep up the Offensive', *An t-Oglach* urged the Volunteers to keep up the pressure against the enemy. 'His strongholds must be attacked, his forces surprised and disarmed, his communication interrupted, his despatches seized, his activities watched, his machinery interfered with, his supplies cut off in every part of the country with such persistence, speed and ubiquity that he will not be able to get his "system" established anywhere.' Orders went out from I.R.A. Headquarters to form 'Flying Columns' and Active Service Units out of the many Volunteers who were on the run. These were the first full-time guerilla bands. Daytime attacks had been uncommon up to this point, as most of the Volunteers were at work and could only be mobilised for night operations. The Flying Columns lived off the country, laid ambushes, carried out raids and took their war into quiet areas which showed a disposition to lead a quiet life, If hard pressed, they hid their arms and melted into the civilian population.

Another force which was to play a notable, and at times notorious, part in the events of the next twelve months was being recruited in London. It was the Auxiliary Division

R.I.C., in which ex-officers with good war records were enrolled as Temporary Cadets. They held a rank equivalent to a sergeant in the R.I.C., and were paid £1 a day with some allowances. Most of them were prepared to go anywhere and do anything from washing up in hotel kitchens to fighting in Mexico. Times were hard for ex-officers, many of whom had hardly been more than schoolboys when they went into the army. They knew no trade but war, and there were few openings for them as civilians, even in humble occupations. An advertisement in the summer of 1920, for example, offering jobs to ten ex-officers to manage street coffee stalls at two pounds ten shillings a week, was answered by five thousand applicants. Fascists were made of such material in other countries.

The first five hundred Auxiliary Cadets, or 'Auxies' as they came to be called, arrived at North Wall Dock, Dublin, at the end of July. They were put through a shortened six-weeks police course at the Curragh training centre, where they learned the difference between a misdemeanour and a felony, and the policeman's power of arrest. These useful pieces of legal knowledge were of little value in guerilla warfare of which they knew and were taught nothing. They received no instruction in motor transport, as it was assumed, falsely, that they were familiar with the internal combustion engine. They did some firing and bombing practice, for which they provided their own instructors. They wore large tam-o'-shanter bonnets with a crowned harp, the emblem of the R.I.C. as a badge. Their tunics, breeches and puttees were khaki, and their accoutrements, consisting of a bandolier across the chest, a belt with a bayonet and scabbard, and an open holster for a revolver on the right thigh, were of black leather. They were later equipped with dark blue uniform and a dark green Balmoral. They were organised into companies of a hundred, and formed a shock force which could be despatched to the areas where the I.R.A. was most active. General

Crozier, a volatile and excitable Irish officer who had lately served with the British Forces in the War of Intervention against Russia in the Baltic States, was sent to Ireland to command this force. The first four companies were despatched to Kilkenny, Cork and to Galway at the end of August.

Over five hundred members of the R.I.C. had resigned in June and July, but the flow of Black and Tans from their recruiting depots in Glasgow and Liverpool, and the small number of Irishmen who were still joining the force, more than made up for the numerical loss. In Dublin Castle, Colonel Winter, who had been sent over from London as Chief of the Combined Intelligence Services, reopened the dried-up channels of information from agents and informers, and began to build an efficient organisation almost from scratch. To the I.R.A. he was soon to become known as 'the holy terror'.

The way to the conference table lay through another twelve months of bloodshed and burning buildings.

CHAPTER SIX

Restoration of Order?

AT THE BEGINNING of August the case of Archbishop Mannix of Melbourne provided a light interlude in Anglo-Irish relations, which also helped to rally opposition to the Government, both at home and abroad. His Grace, a native of Cork, had been speaking on de Valera's platform in the United States, where, among other forthright observations, he told a San Francisco audience, 'Ireland only asked England: "Take one of your hands off my throat and the other out of my pocket."' To a New York audience he said: 'England was never a friend of the United States, and Ireland has the same grievance against the same enemy only ten times greater.' He announced his intention of coming to Ireland to visit his mother, and on the 1st August sailed from New York on the S.S. *Baltic*. An English fellow passenger was roughly handled by over-enthusiastic Irish-Americans who came to wish His Grace Godspeed. Lloyd George had told the House of Commons, five days earlier, 'we have already intimated that, in consequence of his recent utterances, Dr. Mannix will not be allowed to land in Ireland.' Accordingly, on the 8th August, a destroyer intercepted the *Baltic* off Queenstown where the Archbishop intended to disembark, and he was served with a document which informed him that he was free to go anywhere except Ireland, Liverpool, Manchester or Glasgow. He was removed to the destroyer and landed at Penzance, where he observed, with justice: 'The English Government are making themselves look very silly.' The greater part of the Press agreed with him, and *The Times* summed up the general opinion in a leader: 'In the sorry story of Government ineptitude, this treatment of Dr. Mannix may prove to have been by no means the least remarkable chapter.' Catholics everywhere were enraged, and the Irish Hierarchy protested 'against the indignity to the great Archbishop as an invasion of the rights of citizenship and as a procedure provocative of further irritation and unrest the world over'. Lawyers considered this denial of freedom of speech and movement a dangerous precedent. But the Government stood firm against all protests and deputations.

General Macready, at least, was pleased at the 'decision to keep that turbulent priest', as he called Dr. Mannix, 'out of the island, as his appearance in Ireland would have resulted in increased bloodshed', but his absence was also a cause of disturbance. In Dublin many bonfires were lighted on the 9th August in honour of the Archbishop and as a protest against his treatment. A military patrol tried to arrest a group of young men sitting round one of the fires after curfew, and shot and killed one of them. This incident caused an outburst of ill-feeling against the troops in Dublin. Many soldiers were attacked and thrown into the Liffey during the next few days and, finally, a party of soldiers broke out and laid about a hostile crowd with their entrenching tools. They also fired a few shots down the street at the retreating civilians without causing any casualties. The strain on military discipline was enough to make General Macready think it necessary, a few days later, to issue a warning to his troops against looting and reprisals. The General was also anxious that the Black and Tans should be issued with proper police uniforms to avoid confusion with the military. 'The soldiers were subject to quite enough abuse,' he wrote, 'without bearing the supposed sins of the police.'

The Black and Tans were scattered in small detachments over the countryside, and in many areas were practically

17. Before: A detachment of the Gordon Highlanders was detailed to guard wagons containing military stores at Kingsbridge Station, Dublin, in July, 1920. Troops did not always take these duties seriously.

18. After: A few days later, a company of the Dublin Brigade of the I.R.A. surprised and disarmed them and set three wagons on fire in a typical volunteer raid of that time.

19. Cadets of the Auxiliary Division of the Royal Irish Constabulary come to the Curragh camp for training. They are ex-service officers, hold the rank of police sergeant, and are paid £1 a day. They were the most experienced fighters on either side, and soon became the most feared.

20. Sir Hamar Greenwood inspects the Royal Irish Constabulary at their depot in Phoenix Park. He urges them to be disciplined. The constable third from the right, who is still in khaki, is a Black and Tan recruit, as is the man on his right with the incomplete uniform.

confined to their over-crowded barracks. They were under greater stress and less control than the military, and they broke out more often. In the first fortnight of August they wrecked and burned buildings in Roscommon, Galway, Cork, Tipperary, Kerry and Limerick as reprisals for attacks made on them. A party of Black and Tans had also taken a young man called Patrick Lynch from his home in the town of Hospital and shot him. This victim was the first of the Lynches to be killed in mistake for Commandant Liam Lynch of the Irish Republican Army.

On the 13th August the Police Authorities in Dublin Castle published the first issue of a four-page news sheet called *The Weekly Summary*. It was issued free to the police and its purpose was to present the Black and Tans with a more favourable view of the events in Ireland than was provided by most of the local papers, and to keep up their morale with staccato editorials such as the following, which appeared in the third issue:

> They did not wait for the usual uniform
> They came at once.
> They were wanted badly, and the R.I.C.
> Welcome them.
> They know what the danger is.
> They have looked Death in the eyes before,
> and did not flinch.
> They will not flinch now
> They will go on with the job—the job of making
> Ireland once again safe for the law-abiding.
> AND AN APPROPRIATE HELL FOR THOSE WHOSE TRADE
> IS AGITATION AND WHOSE METHOD IS MURDER.

But even the law-abiding found their methods distasteful. Sir Hugh Gratton-Bellew, for example, the Deputy Lieutenant for Galway, resigned his post and his commission as a British magistrate. In a letter to the Lord Chancellor, he wrote: 'I hope my colleagues will follow my example so that the wrecking of Irish towns and the ruin of Irish industry may be proceeded with without any camouflage, or appearance of approval by Irishmen of the sabotage of their country, which retention of office without function would imply.' On the other side, Dermot-Lynch, the member for South-east Cork, resigned from the Dáil with less publicity.

In this context the Government introduced the Restoration of Order in Ireland Bill, which received the Royal Assent on the 9th August. It virtually abolished the principle of trial by jury and established military law. In practice, trial by jury had already fallen into disuse in most areas, as neither witnesses not jury dared attend the courts. Cases of treason, felony and lesser crimes could be tried by court martial. The public could be excluded to safeguard both the members of the court and the witnesses from gunmen. In the cases of crimes punishable by death one member of the court had to be certified by the Lord Chancellor of England or the Lord Chancellor of Ireland as a person of legal knowledge and experience. Military courts of enquiry were substituted for coroners' inquests which commonly found that Sinn Fein victims had been 'wilfully murdered by unknown members of the R.I.C.' and that policemen had died 'of wounds inflicted by some person or persons unknown, whilst bearing arms on behalf of an alien and enemy government'. The Bill had a stormy passage through the House of Commons, where Commander Kenworthy spoke the thought of most of the Opposition when he said, with the exaggeration that is common in the discussion of Irish affairs, there was 'nothing to surpass it in the annals of Irish repressive legislation. It admits the revival of the Star Chamber.'

One of the first prisoners to be tried by court martial under the Restoration of Order in Ireland Act was Terence MacSwiney, Lord Mayor of Cork, member of the Dáil, and Commandant of the First Cork Brigade of the I.R.A. He was another Irish patriot born of an English mother, and had the fanatical zeal for Irish nationalism that this mixture of blood seems so often to engender. He was a brave man, as he was to show, and an utterly ruthless fighter if we are to believe P. S. O'Hegarty, a member of Sinn Fein and the author of *The Victory of Sinn Fein*. In this book the author describes a meeting in May, 1920, with MacSwiney, who made a proposal which, he wrote, 'seemed to me then to be fiendish, and indefensible and inadvisable from every point of view.' It has been suggested that this fearful proposal was for an attack on the troublesome Bishop of Cork. Mac-Swiney was charged with being in possession of a police cipher and of two documents 'likely to cause disaffection to His Majesty'. One of them contained notes for a speech which concluded: 'Facing our enemy we must declare an attitude simply. We see in their régime a thing of evil incarnate. With it there can be no parley—any more than there can be a truce with the powers of Hell. This is our simple resolution—we ask for no mercy and we will make no compromise.' He was sentenced to two years without hard labour. When he was asked if he wished to address the court, he replied: 'I have decided that I shall be free alive or dead within a month, as I will take no food for the period of my sentence', and began the long hunger strike which focused the eyes of the world on Ireland's real and imaginary wrongs, and ended in his death in Brixton Prison seventy-five days later.

Few Irishmen were so uncompromising as Terence MacSwiney, and preparations had been in train since the beginning of August for an Irish Peace Conference to be held in Dublin. The excitement caused by the treatment of Dr. Mannix, the arrest of the Lord Mayor of Cork and the renewed burst of murders and reprisals almost overwhelmed the Conference before it was convened. An R.I.C. constable was shot dead in Limerick on the 15th August. Twenty to thirty Black and Tans, well primed with drink, smashed the windows of houses as people were sitting down to their Sunday dinner, entered some of them to break ornaments and pictures, including, in one house, a portrait of King George V. All Irishmen were 'Shinners' to them. With a motor car loaded with petrol, they tried to set O'Connell Street on fire, reduced two corner houses to rubble, and burned five shops. They killed one of their own number by mistake as well as an English ex-soldier who had served in both the Boer War and the Great War. Another party went to the railway station, dragged an engine driver from his cabin, turned the passengers out of the coaches, fired shots into the air, gave three cheers and drove away.

Times had changed. Five years earlier Lord Wimborne, the Viceroy whom Lord French had succeeded, had entered Limerick to the strains of 'God Save the King' and had driven through streets lined with loyal and cheering Irish citizens. A little group of Sinn Feiners, who had tried on that occasion to stage a counter-demonstration with 'God Save Ireland', had to be saved from the anger of the crowd by the Royal Irish Constabulary who hurried them down a back street.

A District Inspector of the R.I.C. was killed in Templemore, Tipperary, on the next day and Black and Tans set fire to the Town Hall, the Market Hall and to the Urban District Council Offices. The terrified inhabitants fled into the fields. The Black and Tans also burned three co-operative creameries in the district.

A few days later a curious phenomena known as the 'Templemore Miracle' suggested an outbreak of mass hysteria. A young Catholic seminarist saw the statues and holy pictures in the house of a newsagent begin to bleed. Templemore, one of the centres of terror and counter-terror, became a place of pilgrimage. A wave of adventist exultation swept the countryside. The roads to the town were blocked with farm carts, ass carts, outside cars, Fords and bicycles. Such traffic had never been seen, even for the races. Pilgrims slept in the streets and wretches past help were dragged to the newsagent's shop in the hope of a miraculous cure. An old soldier who had been shot through the right knee at the battle of the Somme, regained the use of his leg. A harness-maker was relieved of his sciatica and a girl, in the last stages of consumption, rose from her stretcher and walked. Or so it was said. The police also suspected that a consignment of arms, which had been landed on the West coast, had gone through undetected in the general confusion.

In the North of Ireland, District Inspector Swanzy was assassinated at Lisburn on the 22nd August. He was the man whom the I.R.A. held responsible for the death of Lord Mayor MacCurtain in March. Catholic premises in the town were burnt down as a reprisal and disorder once more spread over the whole of Ulster. Terrified Catholic refugees, who had been driven from their homes in Lisburn, fled to Belfast which had its own problems to face. Rioting had again broken out there and Orange frenzy was once more let loose on 'papists' and on 'rotten prods'. Sixteen men and women had been killed and a prodigious amount of damage caused by looting and arson by the time the troops opened fire to restore order on the 25th August.

The Dublin Peace Conference met on the 24th August in the Antient Concert Rooms in the heady atmosphere of overcharged emotions. The delegates were peers, lieutenants of counties, ex-officers, clergymen, landowners—men of moderation and influence and by no means the creatures of the British Government as some Sinn Feiners imagined. There was Sir Horace Plunkett who saw his life's work for the co-operative Irish agricultural movement going up in flames with the burning of the creameries: The O'Conor Don, a Unionist landowner, who said 'We'll tell Mr. Lloyd George, if the Government don't turn these damned Black and Tans out of the country we'll soon all be damned republicans': Sergeant Hanna, K.C., an Ulsterman, who thought: 'There are the most valid economic reasons why the people of Ulster and Belfast should stand in with their fellow countrymen rather than with the men across the sea.' The Conference urged the immediate release of the Lord Mayor of Cork in a unanimous resolution, and in another called upon 'the Government in the interests of peace, and in order to create a suitable atmosphere for a policy of general appeasement . . . to abate forthwith the stringency of the policy of repression and adopt a policy of amnesty'. The Conference proposed the grant of full nationalist self-government within the Empire and expressed 'its unalterable repugnance to any form of partition of Ireland', though it recognised 'that in any negotiation concerning the relations of North-east Ulster to the rest of Ireland, the former must be accorded the status of a free contracting party'.

These proposals might well have been the basis of negotiation. In London the Cabinet was divided. Winston Churchill, Lord Birkenhead and Walter Long were opposed to any more concessions being made to Ireland; Bonar Law talked wildly of shooting 'half a hundred Sinn Feiners'; the Foreign Secretary, Lord Curzon, insisted that a quick settlement of the Irish problem, by one means or another, was essential to the maintenance of Anglo-American relations and the majority were prepared to back Lloyd George if he dropped the Home Rule Bill for another. But in Ireland the effect of the Black and Tans had been to drive Irishmen to the left: Unionists became Dominion Home Rulers, and Dominion Home Rulers became Sinn Feiners. The idea of any connection with Britain grew to be increasingly repugnant even to moderate men and the men with the guns were determined to make any such settlement impossible.

The widespread hopes for peace dwindled when, in the week after the Peace Conference, the I.R.A. made nearly a thousand raids for arms all over the country. There was rioting in Belfast, and the outlines of a deliberately fostered campaign to drive the Catholic population out of North-east Ulster was clearly discernible. Volunteers enforced the boycott of Ulster goods in the South as a reprisal by turning representatives of Ulster business out of their homes, burning delivery vans and damaging shops. In the course of this campaign three shop assistants were burned to death when a large drapery store was set on fire in Dundalk on the 27th August.

In London, Lord Mayor MacSwiney was reported to be sinking at the end of August. The longshoremen in New York threatened to strike in protest to his imprisonment and the Mayor of New York appealed for his release. The Papal Secretary of State in Rome reported that 300,000 Brazilian Catholics had demanded the Pope's intervention on MacSwiney's behalf. A French paper published front-page headlines of 'Bravo, L'Irlande heroique—Bravo Le Lord Mayor de Cork'. A political commentator explained that it was an Irish custom for a man to die on the threshold of one who has wronged him. A German paper compared him to the legendary Swiss hero, Arnold von Winkelreid, who sacrificed himself for his people. At home, the Society of Friends, and the Labour Party demanded Lord Mayor MacSwiney's release.

The protests continued, and King George V, who was greatly disturbed by the news from Ireland, was also reported to have intervened on his behalf. But Lloyd George, in a statement to the Press on the 25th August, said: 'If the Lord Mayor were released, every hunger striker, whatever his offence, would have to be let off. . . . A complete breakdown of the whole machinery of law and government would follow. Whatever the consequences I cannot take that responsibility.'

It was useless for Bonar Law to reply that since the Lord Mayor's arrest fifteen R.I.C. men had been 'brutally and treacherously done to death without even a chance of defending themselves', and ask: 'Surely the sympathy which has been given in such full measure to the Lord Mayor, whose condition has been brought about by his own deliberate act, is due rather to the bereaved widows and families of the murdered Irish policemen?' He added that the Government fully realised how large a part sentiment played in all human affairs, and, if it were possible, they would gladly take the attitude of the English king who said of an opponent 'He is determined to make himself a martyr, and I am determined to prevent it'. But the Government underestimated the power of sentiment on this occasion, and Mr. Asquith was nearer the mark when he declared: 'The decision to allow the Lord Mayor of Cork to die in prison is a political blunder of the first magnitude.' MacSwiney, the man who was determined to make himself a martyr, said: 'I am confident that my death will do more to smash the British Empire than my release.'

In Cork, eleven prisoners had been hunger striking for two days longer than the Lord Mayor. On the 7th September, the twenty-eighth day of their strike, Alderman Liam de Roiste of Cork, *anglice* William Roche, sent a telegram to the Trade Union Congress: 'Eleven prisoners are dying in Cork prison. Ten are untried and unconvicted. No charge against them. One is twelve months in prison, but is yet unconvicted. Will English Labour let them die?' But the Trade Union Congress was already too pre-occupied with events in Northern Ireland, where eighteen trades unions were involved in the troubles, if only to the extent of having to pay benefit to their members who had been thrown out of work. The Amalgamated Carpenters and Joiners, which had many members in the dockyards, had already sent a deputation to Belfast to explore the possibility of a settlement. By September the anti-Catholic infection had spread to the railwaymen, and the Executive Committee of the National Union of Railwaymen in London passed a unanimous resolution instructing 'the General

Secretary to demand the immediate reinstatement of these
men, with full pay for time lost, also compensation for loss
caused by the household effects of our members being
destroyed'. A fact-finding commission was despatched to
Belfast by the Trade Union Congress, which discovered
that 'the history and traditions of the people of Ireland in
relation to political and religious questions find no parallel
in this country'. It ignored, or failed to observe, that many
Unionist employers were making no efforts to restore the
right to work to 'papists' and to 'rotten prods'. At a loss as
to what to do next, the T.U.C., under the chairmanship of
J. H. Thomas, sent a telegram to the Prime Minister
expressing its horror and indignation at the persecution of
Catholic workers in Belfast, adding: 'We wish to remind
the Government that rebellion was first preached by those
who are condemning to death those others who are fighting
for their country.' The Amalgamated Carpenters and Joiners
alone took any action, and ordered its members not to
work for firms in which Catholic workers were barred. Six
hundred obeyed the Executive, while about two thousand
stayed at work and were expelled from the Union.

British Labour's chief contribution to the cause of the
Irish Republic was indirect. In the late summer of 1920 the
Triple Alliance of miners, railwaymen and transport
workers confronted the Government with the grave threat
of a combined strike. In August, Sir Henry Wilson had
proposed to withdraw four battalions from the Rhine and
ten from Ireland as a precautionary measure to deal with
the possibility of trouble at home. But General Macready
told him that if his forces were reduced to that extent the
whole of the R.I.C. would resign and that he would have
to 'put up the shutters'. Nevertheless, for three months he
was obliged to hold ten battalions ready for instant despatch
to England and seriously limit their usefulness 'just as
troops and police were getting into their stride', he wrote,
'and at a time of the year most favourable to operations'.

He objected to a proposal by the Government that a force of Special Constables should be recruited in Ulster to release troops in the province for service elsewhere, because he felt that, 'as the Constabulary would necessarily be confined to Protestants, it would, unless under the strictest control, probably sow the seeds of civil war between North and South and necessitate the intervention of the Army'. Sir Henry Wilson supported him and wrote: 'Simply to arm a lot of the "Black North" on the chance of their keeping order is childish and worse.' Even so, such a force of Special Constables was enrolled later in the year. They justified Sir Henry's opinion.

The Orangemen were thus unwittingly helping the South by keeping a large number of troops concentrated in the North. The political atmosphere in Belfast was explosive throughout September. Sir James Craig, the Unionist leader, was even afraid that the Orange rank and file would throw off all restraint. They had a paranoiac fear that the Rt. Hon. J. MacMahon, the Catholic Joint Under-Secretary with Sir John Anderson at Dublin Castle, was directing affairs in the North. Accordingly, the Government, at Sir James Craig's suggestion, appointed Sir Ernest Clarke as an additional Assistant Under-Secretary for Belfast. Sir Ernest took up his appointment on the 16th September and set about the problem of getting eight thousand unemployed Catholics back to their jobs. He persuaded the Protestants to abandon their insistence that Catholics should sign a document disclaiming Sinn Fein as a condition of employment, and had opened the way, it seemed, for a general resumption of work. But through ill-timing or a deliberate design to prevent a settlement, the I.R.A. chose this moment to make two attacks on the R.I.C., killing one constable and wounding two others. Three prominent Sinn Feiners were shot in their houses by armed civilians immediately afterwards, and Belfast was once more thrown into confusion by rioting and street fighting. The troops restored order, but the possibility of a return to work by the Catholic dock workers was farther away than ever. Only the members of the Irish Transport Union, of whom nine out of ten were Catholics, were able to hang on grimly to their control of the deep sea docks. In the disturbances from June to December, twenty people had been killed in the rioting in Derry and sixty-two in Belfast.

The outrages in the North helped to bring republican temperatures nearly to boiling point in the South. They were, of course, supposed to have been directly inspired by the vile Saxons represented by the British Government. Sporadic attacks on police and soldiers continued at scattered points over the 26,000 square miles of Southern Ireland, and it would have needed a very much larger concentration of troops than General Macready had at his disposal to stop them.

CHAPTER SEVEN

Reprisals and Protests

BY LATE SEPTEMBER two thousand Black and Tans had reinforced the eight thousand Irishmen still in the regular Royal Irish Constabulary and recruits were coming into Gormanstown, which had recently been made the Black and Tan depot, at the rate of two hundred a week. The police began to move into the offensive and to re-occupy stations from which they had been withdrawn. The newly formed Auxiliary companies, who, according to General Macready, could 'best be described as a pretty tough lot', were already hated and feared. They were the most effective fighting force on either side, ruthless, arrogant and often drunken and violent. They regarded all Irishmen as murderers or 'Shinners'.

In a world beset with war, revolution and industrial unrest, the events in Ireland might well have seemed unimportant, but two much-publicised events on the 20th September both attracted international attention and still further inflamed Irish emotions. In Dublin, an unarmed military ration party called with a lorry at a bakery in Upper Church Street at eleven o'clock to collect bread for the troops. While the soldiers were fetching the bread, four men walking down the street suddenly produced revolvers, shouted to the armed escort to put up their hands and surrender their arms, and at the same time fired, killing one soldier and mortally wounding two others at point-blank range. A second party of Volunteers went into the bakery and wounded one soldier in the ankle and another in the elbow. The N.C.O. in charge ran out of the bakery and armed himself with a rifle. He found an eighteen-year-old medical student, by the name of Kevin Barry, lying under the lorry with an automatic pistol, and arrested him. Kevin Barry was to become the centre of a world-wide agitation almost as great as that provoked by MacSwiney, the hunger-striking Lord Mayor of Cork.

On the evening of the same day, some Volunteers recognised Head Constable Burke of the R.I.C. while he was having a drink with his brother in an hotel in Balbriggan, a village of about two thousand inhabitants twenty miles north of Dublin. They shot Burke dead and wounded his brother. The news quickly reached the Gormanstown depot three miles away. The Black and Tans piled into their tenders and set off on a reprisals raid. They pulled up at the first public house, smashed in the door, broke the windows, seized a quantity of liquor and set fire to the place. They surged through the village singing 'We are the boys of the Bulldog Brigade', shot two men whom they believed rightly or wrongly to be Volunteer officers, burnt three more public houses, a stocking factory which was the property of an English company, nineteen private houses and wrecked a further thirty houses. 'We left Balbriggan and got back to camp about three o'clock in the morning,' a Black and Tan who took part in this raid has recorded. 'There were many sore hearts among us, but there were plenty of bottles to cure them or make them worse.'

The sack of Balbriggan, as it was called, caused indignation both in Ireland and in England. 'It is difficult to believe that the occurrences at Balbriggan can have been entirely the result of a spontaneous outburst of resentment on the part of the incensed policemen,' *The Times* observed. 'There seems to have been behind it a directing influence.' Black and Tan outrages were bad enough for it to be easy to make them appear even worse than they were in reality. In a speech in the House of Commons, Mr. Asquith described the village as looking like a Belgian town that had been wrecked by the Germans in the war, although he had not been to see it himself. An Irish ballad of the time also suggested as much:

> The town of Balbriggan they burnt to the ground
> While the bullets like hailstones were whizzing around.

But most of the damage had been confined to one back street, and it was possible to motor through the village a day or so later without being aware that anything untoward had happened. Some of the inhabitants had profited by the chance to do some burning and looting on their own account during the confusion. On the following Sunday, according to General Macready, 'the parish priest told his congregation they had only got what they deserved'. Whether or not this was true, many of the older priests exercised a restraining influence on their flocks, while some of the younger men threw themselves heart and soul into the I.R.A. struggle.

On the next day a flying column of sixty Volunteers ambushed a tender carrying five Black and Tans near the villages of Ennistymon and Lahinch. As the tender moved up a hill on a sunken road the Volunteers opened concentrated fire at thirty yards range. 'The dead R.I.C. were a gruesome and bloody sight,' one of the attacking party has recorded. They were indeed, for on this, as on other occasions, the I.R.A. used dum-dum bullets. They either did not know or did not care about the Hague Convention which forbade the use of this ammunition. Soldiers and police were on patrol in the area because the police had been warned by an anonymous letter from an informer that an ambush was being planned. 'We would have an easy mind if you would frighten these murderers,' the letter concluded, 'they want more blood.' The police soon came to the grisly scene. Regular R.I.C. men as well as Black and Tans went berserk and drove to the neighbouring village of

Milltown Malbay. They burned eight houses and killed an old man driving a hay cart. They went next to Ennistymon, where they caught a man who was believed to have taken part in the ambush. They shot him, burned four houses and a drapery shop and looted a public house. A twelve-year-old boy was killed while fetching water to put out a fire. The wild and drunken police reached the neighbouring village of Lahinch in the early hours. Most of the inhabitants had taken to the fields. The police set fire to the town hall and to seven houses, in one of which the leader of the ambush was burned alive. A few days later the I.R.A. surprised the police barracks at Trim, captured its arms and equipment and destroyed the building. One constable was wounded. Two hundred Auxiliaries and Black and Tans descended on the town in the small hours and burned and looted homes, shops and public houses.

These outrages rallied Irish opinion and almost the whole of the London Press, with the exception of *The Morning Post*, against the Government. *The Times* fulminated editorially: 'Methods, inexcusable even under the loose code of revolutionaries, are certainly not methods which the government of Great Britain can tolerate on the part of its servants.' *The Daily News* reported: 'The suspicion is rapidly growing in this country and abroad that British authority is secretly conniving at the barbarous reprisals now being systematically carried out.' In a letter to that newspaper, Major General F. Maurice wrote that the result of the creation of the Black and Tans 'has been to increase the number of murders. It has produced a peculiarly revolting form of guerilla warfare in which the chief sufferers are women and children. This must be stopped at once. The way to stop it is to disband the Black and Tans.' General Sir Hubert Gough wrote to *The Manchester Guardian:* 'I don't think any truthful or sane person can avoid the conclusion that the authorities are deliberately encouraging and, what is more, actually screening reprisals and "counter murder" by the armed forces of the Crown.' The farther away from the scene of action, the worse the reprisals seemed, and *Le Matin* in Paris informed its readers that 'never since the Middle Ages has such savage brutality been recorded'.

The objections to reprisals were not all inspired by humanitarian motives. Sir Henry Wilson, for example, noted in his diary on the 29th September:

'I had 1½ hours this evening with Lloyd George and Bonar Law. I told them what I thought of reprisals by the "Black and Tans", and how this must lead to chaos and ruin. Lloyd George danced about and was angry, but I never budged. I pointed out that these reprisals were carried out without anyone being responsible; men were murdered, houses burnt, villages wrecked (such as Balbriggan, Ennistymon, Trim, etc.). I said that this was due to want of discipline, and this *must* be stopped. It was the business of the Government to govern. If these men ought to be murdered, then the Government ought to murder them. Lloyd George danced at all this, said no Government could possibly take this responsibility. After much wrangling, I still sticking to it that either these things ought to be done or ought not, and if they ought then it was the business of the Government to do them, and if they ought not then they ought to be stopped, I got some sense into their heads, and Lloyd George wired for Hamar Greenwood, Macready, Tudor and others to come over tomorrow night.

'I warned Lloyd George that, although up to now the army had remained disciplined and quiet, it was quite possible that they might break out any minute if one of their officers were murdered by Sinn Feiners, and that the report tonight that Mallow had been sacked after the murder of one of the sergeants of the 17th Lancers may well prove to be that the 17th Lancers had sacked the

21. Templemore, Tipperary, had the unpleasant distinction of being set on fire as reprisal by both the Black and Tans and the military. In August, 1920, Black and Tans burned the Town Hall, Market Hall, and Urban District Council Offices after the assassination of a District Inspector. Two months later, men of the Northamptonshire Regiment ran amok after an ambush. On this occasion Black and Tans restrained the troops, and were publicly thanked by the Local Council, whose offices they had burned.

22. A Strange Interlude: In the middle of a campaign of ambushes and reprisals, a Catholic seminarist saw holy statues in a Templemore shop bleeding. The halt and the maimed flocked to the scene of the 'Templemore Miracle'. The Church was non-committal; the police sceptical; and the I.R.A. delighted that the crowds of pilgrims made it impossible for police and military transport to move.

23. Left: The postman continues his round unmoved while members of the Cumann na m'Ban, or Irishwomen's Council, wave to prisoners at the upper windows of Mountjoy Gaol from the top of a cab. Such excitements are nothing to speak of in Dublin in 1920. Cumann na m'Ban provided nurses and couriers and arranged 'safe' houses for men 'on the run'.

24. Below: Three Auxiliaries stand on guard at a military sports meeting in the grounds of King George's Hospital, Dublin. The Auxiliaries could 'best be described as a pretty tough lot' in General Macready's view, and, according to an I.R.A. commander, seemed to many Volunteers to be 'super fighters and all but invincible'. Many had been decorated for gallantry in the Great War.

town. All this was terribly dangerous. What was evident to me after this long talk was that neither Lloyd George nor Bonar Law had the faintest idea of what to do.'

Sir Henry Wilson's fears were justified. A detachment of twenty men of the Cork No. 2 Brigade had made a daring and well-planned raid on the Mallow Barracks under the command of Liam Lynch. They waited until the main body of troops had left for their morning's exercise, then rushed the place, killed the sergeant in charge, rounded up the few soldiers left behind on fatigues and locked them up in one of the stables. They captured twenty-seven rifles, two light machine guns and a considerable quantity of ammunition. Later in the evening troops scoured the town, yelling like savages, firing into the air and setting light to houses of Sinn Fein supporters, Nationalists and Unionists alike. They burned the town hall, a creamery which employed three hundred people, a small hotel and many shops. The terrified townspeople rushed through the streets, many with children in their arms, some to find sanctuary in the convent schools and some to spend the night in the safety of a cemetery. Black and Tans, on this occasion, tried to restrain the troops. They helped to put out fires and find shelter for the homeless. In spite of the confusion, no one was killed. In England, *The Times* once more summed up the general feeling of the Press: 'Day by day the tidings from Ireland grow worse. The accounts of arson and destruction by the Military at Mallow as a revenge for the Sinn Fein raid which caught the 17th Lancers napping, must fill English readers with a sense of shame. . . .The name of England is being sullied throughout the Empire and throughout the world by this savagery for which the Government can no longer escape, however much they may seek to disclaim responsibility.'

The Coalition Cabinet was still divided and a majority was urging Lloyd George to find a settlement. But in

Ireland, Sinn Fein was in no mood to accept anything less than complete surrender to its terms, and the Dáil could not have stopped the I.R.A. even if it had wanted to. Reprisals had not turned all Irishmen into Republicans as the O'Conor Don feared, but they made many, previously neutral, people hate the name of England. Reprisals also provoked some members of the I.R.A. to acts of insensate savagery. On the day the Black and Tans ran wild in Ennistymon, Lahinch and Miltown Malbay, for example, a party of Volunteers a few miles away buried a Resident Magistrate up to his neck in sand, just below high water mark, as they imagined. He had been kidnapped and condemned to death as a traitor, but the appointed executioner had wounded him in the head without killing him. The Volunteers returned the next day to find the victim still alive. They dug him out and buried him again farther down the beach, where he could watch the next tide advance, to put him slowly out of his long agony.

Violence begat violence as ever, and by the end of September the Black and Tans had earned such a reputation for keeping order that when it was announced that some of them were going to be stationed at Drogheda, the scene of one of Oliver Cromwell's Irish massacres, mill owners checked their fire-fighting equipment, the mill girls anticipated a winter of unemployment and the local R.I.C. said they would refuse to work with their reinforcements. The Black and Tans arrived, nevertheless, and let the citizens know what to expect in the following proclamation

DROGHEDA BEWARE

If in the vicinity a policeman is shot, five of the leading Sinn Feiners will be shot.

It is not coercion—it is an eye for an eye.

We are not drink-maddened savages as we have been described in the Dublin rags. We are not out for loot.

We are inoffensive to women. We are as humane as other Christians, but we have restrained ourselves too long.

Are we to lie down while our comrades are being shot in cold blood by the corner boys and ragamuffins of Ireland?

We say 'Never', and all the inquiries in the world will not stop our desire for revenge.

Stop the shooting of police, or we will lay low every house that smells of Sinn Fein.

Remember Balbriggan.

(By Order) Black and Tans.

Without excusing Black and Tan outrages, it must be remembered that the provocation was often very great. On the last day of September fifty Volunteers ambushed a lorry near the village of Tubercurry in Sligo. District Inspector Brady, R.I.C., an ex-Irish Guards officer and an honourable and popular man who had kept his men under firm discipline, was killed by three terrible wounds from expanding bullets. A constable had the calf of one leg blown off by another of these bullets and a third had his face peppered with gun-shot pellets. The lorry, however, drove through to the police post at Tubercurry. A party of sixteen Black and Tans and ten soldiers with an officer arrived from Sligo to investigate in the evening. Once more they went berserk. A police officer tried to restrain his men, but they set fire to three shops and damaged several others before they could be brought under control. A little later two police parties went out to the Tubercurry Creamery, half a mile out of the town, and burnt it to the ground.

On the same day Sir Hamar Greenwood addressed a parade of the Royal Irish Constabulary at their depot in Phoenix Park as follows:

'You are a disciplined force, and I confidently count upon you to maintain that discipline, no matter what the provocation. Accounts of reprisals in certain newspapers are always misleading, and frequently misrepresent acts of justifiable self-defence as reprisals, but there are cases in which unjustifiable action has undoubtedly been taken. These cases are being carefully investigated. Meanwhile it is necessary to repeat and to emphasise that reprisals will ruin the discipline of the force, and can not be countenanced by those in authority. The great provocation under which men suffer who see their comrades and friends brutally murdered is fully recognised, and by no one more than myself; but the police are urged to maintain, in spite of this, that self-control that has characterised the force in the past.'

Sir Hamar was no doubt sincere in his detestation of these reprisals, and quite correct when he told a London paper in an interview, 'the number of reprisals is few and the damage done is exaggerated'. Sinn Fein propaganda was brilliantly organised. English and foreign journalists were taken regularly for a tour of what was known in Dublin Castle as 'the Republican scenic railway'. One correspondent, on calling on an officer at the Castle before returning home, was surprised to be told the itinerary he had followed.

'You went to Kilteragh, the home of Sir Horace Plunkett, and you had a couple of hours with George Russell at Plunkett House. Desmond Fitzgerald called on you at the Shelbourne Hotel, and with an elaborate show of secrecy arranged an interview with Arthur Griffith. One or two harmless young Catholic priests fell into conversation with you at the Shelbourne. You had invitations to tea from Mrs. Erskine Childers, Maud Gonne MacBride and Mrs. Stopford Green, who described atrocities they claim to have seen. Then you went to Thurles to see the Archbishop of

Cashel, and from there with a letter of introduction to the O'Rahilly in Cork, where you also had a talk with Florrie, the porter of the Imperial Hotel. Then you went to Limerick to see Mr. Stephen O'Mara.' Many of the books, pamphlets and articles of the period show signs of this combined influence. In particular, the opinions of Florrie the porter, a man of moderate, but pithily expressed, nationalist views, reached a wide reading public all over the world under various correspondents' names.

The propagandists had plenty to work on. The issue of Dublin Castle's newssheet for the police, *The Weekly Summary*, for example, which was published a few days after Sir Hamar Greenwood's condemnation of reprisals, could hardly be said to preach the restraint that he insisted upon so strongly. Among other items, it contained an article entitled 'The First Reprisal', which was an account of the origin of 'the murder campaign', and concluded with an emotional description of the shooting in an ambush of 'a cheery Irish boy' who had joined the R.I.C. 'Big men with big hearts but gentle hands did what they could, but the young life ebbed away. . . . The grim, pale, determined faces gazed down on the corpse of their young comrade. That night occurred the first reprisal.' An extract from a proclamation by General Paine, Federal Commander in Western Kentucky in the American Civil War, was printed in italics: '*I shall shoot every guerilla taken in my district, and if your Southern brethren retaliate by shooting a Federal soldier, I will walk out five of your rich bankers, and cotton men, and make you kneel down and shoot them. I will do it, so help me God.*' An extract from *The Morning Post* headed 'An Anti-Sinn Fein Society. Two lives for one threatened' was reprinted without comment. It recorded the circulation of the following notice in Cork: 'At a specially convened meeting of the All-Ireland Anti-Sinn Fein Society held in Cork on this 11th day of October, 1920, we, the Supreme Council of the Cork Circle, have reluctantly decided that, if in the future any member of His Majesty's Forces be murdered, two members of the Sinn Fein party in the County of Cork will be killed. And in the event of a member of the Sinn Fein party not being available, three sympathisers will be killed. This will apply equally to laity and clergymen of all denominations. In the event of a member of His Majesty's Forces being wounded, or an attempt made to wound him, one member of the Sinn Fine party will be killed, or if a member of the Sinn Fein party is not available, two sympathisers will be killed.'

Cork, where this notice appeared, competed with Dublin for the honour of being the centre of the I.R.A.'s campaign against the Crown Forces. On the 24th September an I.R.A. ambush nearly bagged General Strickland, the Commander of the forces in Cork, while he was motoring to the quay to go on a month's leave. He ordered the immediate arrest of a dozen prominent members of Sinn Fein, to keep the troops busy and prevent another outburst like the sacking of Mallow. 'Had Strickland been killed,' General Macready wrote, 'no power on earth would have restrained the troops from taking their toll of vengeance on the town.'

In Dublin, Michael Collins had identified the members of what the I.R.A. called the 'Dublin Castle Murder Gang'. They were the counterpart of his own 'Squad' of assassins. One of the 'Murder Gang's' victims, John A. Lynch, a business man from Kilmallock, had been shot dead in the Exchange Hotel on the 23rd September in yet another attempt to despatch Liam Lynch. It was the wrong man, but he was as dead as Cinna the poet who is killed for Cinna the politician in *Julius Cæsar*. Military terrorists are often misinformed, as the British Army was to discover many years later in Palestine. On the 1st October Arthur Griffith announced to a party of international journalists that a number of Sinn Fein leaders had been listed for assassination by British agents. 'I am the first on the list,' he said, 'and the story is to be circulated, as it was in the case of the Lord Mayor of Cork, that I was assassinated because I was urging moderate action. The same tools are to be used as were used on Tuesday night week to assassinate Mr. Lynch in his hotel.'

In the three months July to September, 1920, the Crown Forces had lost fifty-four police and twelve soldiers killed. One hundred police and fifty-four soldiers had been wounded, and forty-nine police and eighty soldiers disarmed; thirty-three court houses had been destroyed and seventeen damaged; eight defended barracks had been destroyed, four damaged and twenty unsuccessfully attacked. There had been twenty-five raids on coastguard stations and two on light-houses, and three hundred and twenty-five cases of arson, mostly on unoccupied houses belonging to Unionists as reprisals for reprisals. In many parts of the country the I.R.A. had almost used up its stock of Unionist houses to burn. The Volunteers had been in action, in one way or another, on nearly three thousand occasions. In the same period, the propagandist *Irish Bulletin* claimed that Crown Forces, police and military, had shot up or wrecked and burned property on nearly seventy different occasions and had been responsible for fifty-four deaths. On these figures the I.R.A. could, and did, claim to be winning.

By wartime standards, if this was a war, the casualties were not heavy. In these three months, for example, over four hundred British soldiers had been killed and over a thousand wounded in Mesopotamia. But people in England did not regard the events in Ireland as war, and were shocked at the policy of irresponsible reprisals carried out by their own countrymen. The Conservative Lord Robert Cecil, who had voted for the Restoration of Order in Ireland Act, was appalled at the disorderly behaviour of the police, and did not believe that reprisals could make rebels less rebellious. Lord Grey thought that 'the government of Ireland has never been such a reproach or discredit to British statesmanship as it is today'. The Labour Party prepared a demand for an inquiry into the practice of reprisals. Mr. Asquith again advocated the immediate granting of Dominion status to Ireland—a proposal which de Valera immediately rejected in advance during an interview in New York. Nevertheless, rumours of peace once more spread through the political clubs in London. But on the 10th October Lloyd George extinguished all hope of an early settlement in a speech which rejected the idea of Dominion status for Ireland and dealt at length with the necessity of 'breaking up the murder gangs' and even justified reprisals. 'The police naturally feel that the time has come to defend themselves and that is what is called reprisals in Ireland,' he said. Sinn Fein could not have it both ways. If they were at war they must expect the consequences. 'You cannot have a one-sided war.'

Two days later, Dan Breen, the man who had opened hostilities at Soloheadbeg Quarry in 1919, was nearly caught in Dublin in what a Sinn Fein writer has called 'one of the most dramatic combats of the war'. Two intelligence officers were raiding the house of a certain Professor Carolan who was suspected of harbouring men on the run. One of the officers was the brother of Colonel Smyth, who had been killed in Cork. They knocked on the door of a room in which Dan Breen was sheltering with Séan Treacy, another well-known gunman who had also been at Soloheadbeg. The gunmen fired through the door, killing both officers. The soldiers of the picket, which was supposed to be surrounding the house, rushed in when they heard the shots, killed Professor Carolan, thinking he was a gunman, then broke in the door to find the window open and the men gone. They had fallen into a conservatory below and blood trails showed that both men had been cut by the glass. Dan Breen gives a more exciting account of these events in his book *My Fight for Irish Freedom*. He writes:

'The house had been surrounded by hundreds of troops. I had driven them off from the landing, and when trying to escape from the window was met with a shower of bullets, a few of them struck me—but a couple of wounds or so didn't matter. Treacy had already got away, and after I had dropped through the roof of the conservatory, in the clear moonlight I could discern countless steel helmets all round the house. The Tommies were blazing away at me; but clinging with one hand to the greenhouse and with the other to my German pistol I sought a mark on the enemy—and within a minute not a soldier could be seen.'

His further adventures that night included, in his own account, fighting his way past another group of soldiers and an armoured car, and then scaling an eighteen-foot wall in spite of five serious wounds, several lesser wounds and a broken toe. His injuries, fortunately, proved to be very much less serious when he reached hospital. Davy Crockett could not have done better nor Sir John Falstaff have spun so glorious a tale. Treacy was killed three days later when firing at an Intelligence Officer. This brave young gunman, the son of a small Tipperary farmer, was described by Breen as 'the greatest military genius of our race'. It is not often that an Irish myth can so easily be traced to its source.

On the 20th October the Labour leader, Mr. Arthur Henderson, moved a Resolution in the more prosaic surroundings of the House of Commons: 'That this house regrets the present state of lawlessness in Ireland and the lack of discipline in the armed forces of the Crown, resulting in the death or injury of innocent citizens and the destruction of property: and is of the opinion that an independent investigation should at once be instituted into the cause, nature and extent of reprisals on the part of those whose duty is the maintenance of law and order.' Sir Hamar

Greenwood replied for the Government in a discursive and emotional speech. He assured the House:

I have laid down a code of still more severe discipline for the Royal Irish Constabulary, and I shall be glad to know that it will meet with approval. I myself had a parade of a large number of the Royal Irish Constabulary. I addressed them. I saw that what I said was published in nearly every paper in Ireland. . . . I put the matter in as strong words as I could command that their business, and mine, was to prevent crime and to detect criminals, and when there was great provocation they must not give way. But I cannot in my heart of hearts—and, Mr. Speaker, I say this—it may be right or it may be wrong—I cannot condemn in the same way those policemen who lost their heads as I condemn the assassins who provoked this outrage. . . .The best and the surest way to stop reprisals is to stop the murder of policemen, soldiers and loyal citizens. I regret these reprisals beyond words. It is a reflection on the discipline of a famous force. It is a reflection on my administration as political head of that force. But if I could bring to the minds and hearts ot every member of this House—I do not care on whaf Benches they sit—the two years of agony, of the intolerable provocation that these policemen, and some cases soldiers, have gone through, the situation would be better understood, and reprisals, whilst condemned, and properly condemned, would also be understood.

The House of Commons, largely composed of members who were known at the time as 'the hard-faced business men who had done well out of the war', rejected the Labour resolution by 346 votes to 74. They saw Sinn Fein as another form of 'Bolshevism'—a problem with which they were much obsessed at home and abroad. A coal strike had started two days earlier, and twenty thousand unemployed rioting in Whitehall on the same day suggested that revolution might be round the corner. *The Morning Post* probably summed up the feeling of the majority in its leader the following morning: 'Whatever we may think of these reprisals in theory, in practice they are found to be the most effective way of causing these murders to cease.' It was possible to defend the policy of reprisals, or to deny that it existed. Lloyd George had followed the first course at Caernarvon and Sir Hamar Greenwood the second in the House of Commons, causing Lord Hugh Cecil to observe: 'It seems to be agreed that there are no such things as reprisals, but they are having a good effect.'

On the day of the debate, Terence MacSwiney lost consciousness. It was the seventieth day of his hunger strike in Brixton Gaol, and a doctor administered food and brandy. His long ordeal had been followed with awe and curiosity. There was a rumour that he had been taking nourishment, secretly carried into the prison in the voluminous black beard of Father Dominic who was attending him. Mr. Eustice Miles, the vegetarian food reformer, thought such incredulity merely showed 'how little the public realises the benefits of fasting'. In Cork the I.R.A. threatened reprisals if he were allowed to die, and sent a warning message to R.I.C. Barracks:

> If Lord Mayor dies
> Resign if wise.
> > O.C. Cork.

In Dublin Kevin Barry was tried on the same day at a court martial in Marlborough Barracks, and sentenced to death for killing a soldier, in the attack on the ration party of the 20th September. An appeal for a reprieve on account of his youth was rejected on the grounds that the dead soldier was only a year older, and that the I.R.A. in Cork had recently killed two seventeen-year-old soldiers in Cork. Two drummer boys of the Manchester Regiment, aged thirteen and fourteen, were later to hold the melancholy record of being the youngest service victims on either side. Arthur Griffith appealed to the civilised world through *The Irish Bulletin* for action to save Kevin Barry's life, and Erskine Childers opened a campaign on his behalf in a vigorous letter to the British Press.

But Barry was momentarily forgotten in the drama of the Lord Mayor of Cork's last hours. He died at 5.40 a.m. on the 25th October. The British Press, from left to right, expressed a shocked reverence. *The Daily Herald* wrote: 'The Lord Mayor of Cork is dead. He has his reward— the reward of Christ-like service to liberty, the highest of human ideals.' And *The Daily Telegraph*: 'The Lord Mayor of Cork condemned himself to death for the sake of a cause in which he passionately believed, and it is impossible for men of decent instincts to think of such an act unmoved.' On the 28th October his funeral procession made its two-hour journey from St. George's Cathedral, Southwark, to Euston through streets lined with silent and respectful Londoners. The funeral cortège was preceded by mounted policemen followed by a detachment of the I.R.A. in uniform, a kilted pipe band playing *Goodbye to Cork* and a posse of priests led by Archbishop Mannix. 'I want you to bear witness that I die as a soldier of the Irish Republic,' were MacSwiney's last words. This brave Anglo-Irishman had chosen to die on the strangest of battle fields in the strangest of wars.

In Dublin, General Macready was alarmed to learn that the mourners intended 'to bring the body to Dublin, and thence, in what would have been worked up into a triumphal progress, to Cork, a proposal I successfully opposed, as if carried out it would have led to rioting on a scale difficult to foresee.' He gave orders that the body was to be taken direct to Cork. There were angry scenes at Holyhead when this decision became known. Miss Annie MacSwiney, the dead man's sister, clung to the coffin and the mourning party, seventy-five strong, made a defensive ring round her.

The police, after an undignified scuffle, finally managed to secure the coffin, and a detachment of Black and Tans earned more odium for the Force by taking it on board and were followed by angry shouts of 'body snatchers'.

The day of the funeral, the 29th October, passed quietly and *The Irish Bulletin* reported, on the next day, that 'the response to Dáil Eireann's call for the observance of yesterday as a day of mourning was complete in every respect.' The response was not surprising. A tradesman who refused to shut his shop in Borris, County Carlow, on that day was boycotted. He later took legal action, and both he and his solicitor were shot. Terror was a more powerful influence than the moral authority of the Dáil. After the burial of Terence MacSwiney, public interest switched back to Kevin Barry. Few people in England imagined that the sentence would be carried out. On the 31st October the Archbishop of Dublin and the Lord Mayor appealed to General Macready, to Sir John Anderson and Lloyd George to spare his life. The pressure of public opinion and the knowledge that his death could heighten feeling against the Administration had already persuaded Lloyd George, Sir Hamar Greenwood, the Viceroy and General Macready that it would be wise to commute the sentence on grounds of expediency if not humanity, but the Inspector-General of the R.I.C. threatened to resign if Kevin Barry were reprieved. He was accordingly hanged on the morning of the 1st November, to join the ranks of Ireland's martyrs and to have a street named after him in Dublin.

In the House of Commons, J. H. Thomas spoke of him as 'a studious boy loved by everyone who knew him, brave and educated'. He declared that Sir Henry Wilson was responsible for his actions and death because he (Sir Henry) had championed the cause of Ulster's resistance to the Home Rule Bill in 1914, and had read an affidavit which Kevin Barry had sworn in prison that he had his hair pulled and his arm twisted under interrogation.

Despite Sir Hamar Greenwood's assurances, the reprisal campaign had gathered momentum throughout October. After an unsuccessful attack on a police patrol in Roscommon, Black and Tans had set out on a burning spree, ravaging small farms in the neighbourhood, stopping at one house to lecture a school mistress on the wickedness of Sinn Feiners and, while they soaked the stairs and woodwork in petrol telling her that they would shoot her husband when they found him. In Galway, leading citizens had sent their wives and children away as bombing shops and houses was part of the Black and Tans' evening entertainment on pay nights. On the 18th October, three lorry loads of R.I.C. went to the Abbeydorney Creamery, five miles from Tralee; they smashed the windows, clubbed the manager with a rifle, took 3 cwt. of butter, 240 lb. of cheese and set the place alight with petrol. On the 30th October five policemen were killed and two kidnapped near Tralee, and Black and Tans set the town hall on fire. The military intervened and cordoned off the police while the fire-brigade extinguished the flames. On the same night thirty men of the Northamptonshire Regiment broke out in Templemore after an ambush. They raided a spirit grocer's and burned it down, looted a draper's shop and, dressed up in women's blouses, raged through the town, burning and looting as they went. On this occasion the R.I.C. and the Black and Tans intervened to restore order and were thanked by the local Council. Black and Tans tried to set a creamery on fire near Listowel because a girl had had her hair cropped for walking out with one of their number. They themselves cropped the hair of two other girls and beat up six men. As many as half a dozen outrages of this kind occurred almost daily in scattered parts of the south and west. Police or soldiers were killed or attacked and civilians were made to suffer for it.

By the end of October nine companies of Auxiliaries were stationed in Kilkenny, Limerick, Cork, Galway, Mayo,

Clare, Dublin, Meath and Kerry. Each company was equipped with two Ford cars and six Crossley tenders which made them an effective mobile force. In theory they were under the control of the County Inspector of the R.I.C., but, in fact, little restraint was put upon their activities, and not nearly enough by their commanding officers. Five company commanders had resigned since the first companies of Auxiliaries had been sent out in August, and the problem of keeping them under discipline was one that was never entirely solved. Sir Hamar Greenwood stated in the House of Commons on the 20th October: 'I have yet to find one authentic case of a member of those auxiliary forces being accused of anything wrong,' at a time when fifty had already been dismised for various irregularities. One of them, an ex-major with the D.S.O., had returned to Ireland and enjoyed a successful two months as a motor-car bandit before he was caught, tried and sentenced. On the day after Sir Hamar's statement three lorry loads of Auxiliaries drew up outside a public house in Moycullen, County Galway, ordered a number of young men out, removed the jackets of half, the trousers of the rest and then thrashed them. One boy had his nose smashed by a rifle butt. During a night raid in Clare a party of Auxiliaries with blackened faces put a halter round a young man's neck, took down his trousers and thrashed him saying, 'You've had your day. We are going to have ours now.' Such outbursts of sadism often generated more hatred and fury than did reprisals.

There was an ugly mood on both sides in the autumn of 1920. History is notorious for not repeating itself, but there are interesting parallels between Ireland in 1920 and Cyprus in 1958. In both countries a legitimate movement for self-determination degenerated into gun law, into senseless killing for the sake of killing. Both islands were considered to be strategically essential to British interests. The war party in the Cabinet thought that they could be best secured by a firm policy of repression and the offer of a solution that was unacceptable to nationalist feeling. The die-hards, on both occasions, raised the cry of 'no surrender', and the moderates argued that a freely negotiated settlement was the only safeguard. At moments when agreement seemed close, a local commander in Ireland boasted of his intention 'to wipe the swine out', and another in Cyprus claimed to have the 'bastards on the run'. The harder the Crown Forces hit back, the more they united a naturally friendly people against them in hatred, if not in active resistance, and, in both countries, courts found strangely, that there was no evidence to incriminate the Crown Forces when prisoners in custody died of injuries. Crown Forces broke out and took the law into their own hands in both islands, but less frequently and with very much less publicity in Cyprus. The Irish and Cypriot leaders, with whom the Government had to deal, were first interned and later left at liberty, while young Irishmen and Cypriots were ill-advisedly executed to make martyrs for their respective causes. There are differences. In Cyprus, the Turks could only create some of the difficulties caused by the Ulstermen in Ireland, and at home the conscience of the British public has become markedly less sensitive during the intervening years.

25. 20th September, 1920. The 'sack of Balbriggan', as it was called, by Black and Tans, focused world attention on the campaign of reprisals. The Prime Minister, Lloyd George's defence of this policy in one speech and the Chief Secretary, Sir Hamar Greenwood's denial of it in another did nothing to reassure British public opinion.

26. A little earlier on the same day, Volunteers of the Dublin Brigade of the I.R.A. attacked an unarmed military ration party outside a bakery, and killed one young soldier and mortally wounded two others. One of the assailants, Kevin Barry, an eighteen-year-old Irish medical student, was arrested, and a crowd immediately converged upon the scene in Upper Church Street to discuss the event, and, as so often in Dublin at that time, magnify it by rumour. Kevin Barry was later tried and hanged.

27. In a typical I.R.A. operation ten days later, a company of the Meath Brigade rushed the Royal Irish Constabulary's barracks at Trim, early on a Sunday morning when the majority of the garrison was at mass. They surprised and overpowered the eight men left in the building, wounding a sergeant severely. They collected the arms and ammunition and set the building on fire.

Cashman, Dublin.

28. Lord Mayor Terence MacSwiney comes home to his last resting place in Cork after his seventy-five day hunger strike. His dramatic death has created world-wide sympathy for the Irish cause.

29. Go anywhere? Do anything? The prospect at home for many young ex-officers like these Auxiliary cadets guarding the Mansion House Dublin was unemployment or casual labour.

CHAPTER EIGHT

'Bloody Sunday'

IN THE AUTUMN of 1920, an Irishman, if asked what he thought of the 'murder gang', could justifiably ask: 'Which one?' Nearly every night men were taken out of their beds and shot by one side or the other. Police and soldiers were trigger-happy and on the 1st November, the day Kevin Barry was hanged, Black and Tans in a wild burst of firing, killed a woman sitting on a wall with a child in her arms at Gort in County Galway. 'It was the sort of unfortunate accident that happens in war.' Lloyd George explained later in the House of Commons. In war? The Opposition pressed the point home. The Government had denied that there was a war in Ireland. They were dealing with 'murder gangs'. 'It is a war on their side,' Lloyd George replied. 'It is a rebellion.'

Another of the unfortunate accidents that happen in war occurred a few days later in Dublin when a lorry load of soldiers, firing at a group of youths who dispersed and ran away, killed two small girls. A pamphlet entitled *Sinn Fein and the Irish Volunteers* was issued to all troops in October. It urged them to be disciplined, vigilant and suspicious:

'Every soldier in Ireland must realise that the most harmless-looking civilian may be armed and hostile, that he has cunning and desperate men to deal with who will stop at nothing, and are capable of committing any outrage—provided the risk to themselves is not great, but who, if stood up to, generally consider that discretion is the better part of valour.'

The death of the Lord Mayor of Cork had aroused world-wide interest in, and sympathy for, the cause of the Irish Republic. The slightest incident was fully reported, frequently in exaggerated form, to bring news of British infamy to readers in distant countries who, until then, had never even heard of Ireland. At the beginning of November the little town of Tralee was in the news. Two constables had been kidnapped in the attack in which five Black and Tans had been killed on the 30th October; the soldiers, who had intervened to stop the rioting on that night, had withdrawn, and on the next day Black and Tans set about the place with hatchets, crowbars, petrol and bombs. They plastered the walls with a message which read: 'Take notice that all business premises, shops, etc., in Tralee must be kept closed and work suspended until such time as the police in Sinn Fein custody are returned. Anyone disobeying this order will be dealt with in a drastic manner.' The town was in a state of seige and, at the end of the week, many people were on the verge of starvation. A French correspondent reported: 'I do not remember even during the war having seen people so profoundly terrified as those of this little town of Tralee.' Bakeries were allowed to open on the 8th November, and on the 9th the military took over and posted up a notice: 'Business may be resumed in Tralee tomorrow in view of the hardships imposed on loyal subjects. Other means will be resorted to for the recovery of the two police in Sinn Fein custody. Public houses will remain open until the usual hour.' There were few loyal subjects left in Tralee, and the two missing Black and Tans were past recovery: they had been thrown alive into a gas retort and burned to death.

The tempo of murder and reprisal was meanwhile accelerated. During the first week of November ten constables and three soldiers were killed and twenty-four constables and one soldier wounded. On the 4th November, Granard, in Longford, was burned, sacked and looted by

Black and Tans after the assassination of a District Inspector. There were no casualties because the inhabitants knew, by this time, what to expect and had evacuated the town. On the 9th November, Lloyd George announced, in a speech in the Guildhall, that 'we have taken steps by which we have murder by the throat'. On the following day there was a Cabinet meeting on Ireland. 'I was not sent for,' Sir Henry Wilson wrote in his diary, 'but they thought everything was going on so well in Ireland, i.e., government by "Black and Tans", that they would leave it at that and not take over reprisals by government action.' Over in Ireland, his brother, James Mackay Wilson, the Deputy Lieutenant of Longford, received a visit from the blacksmith of Ballinalee, later General Séan McKeon, who was the hero of a night engagement in which a flying column ambushed a convoy of eleven lorries coming from the sacking of Granard. The General, then Vice-Brigadier of the Longford I.R.A., ordered James Wilson to write to his brother and tell him that if reprisals did not stop, his house would be burned and that he would probably die with it. The letter was not written and the threat was not executed.

The sporadic ambushes and assassination of police, and occasionally of soldiers, were presented to the world as evidence that Ireland was a nation in arms against the English oppressors. The few hundred active members of the I.R.A. were not deceived by their own propagandists; they were well aware that the majority of Irish people wanted peace, and they were acutely anxious about how much more the non-belligerent population would stand. Michael Collins could write to *The Gaelic American* for the record, and deny that there was a moderate element in the I.R.A. which wanted peace, but at the time, one of his chief preoccupations was how to get Volunteer commanders, who had been issued with arms, to use them. In some districts, Black and Tans were even allowed to play with children, in spite of the boycott of the police, and were welcomed because their presence saved young men from being forced into the I.R.A. The shooting was limited to very few areas.

The Irish railway workers, who for six months had been accepting dismissal rather than carry troops or munitions, put up a less publicised, but much more impressive resistance that might well have been an example to their fellow countrymen. The Irish railways were being brought to a gradual standstill through the shortage of engine drivers. In mid-November, an All-Ireland Labour Congress met in the Mansion House to consider a situation that was causing more hardship to the Irish than inconvenience to the Crown Forces, but, with two dissentients, they decided to continue the struggle. The women members were particularly resolute and insisted that half Ireland would gladly starve to make England 'feel the hunger pinch'. Irish women were commonly much more militant than Irishmen at this time, and members of the *Cumann na m'Ban*, or Irishwomen's Council, alarmed their men with their enthusiastic talk of the necessity for slaughter and sacrifice far more than they alarmed their enemies.

There was often more sound than fury in Republican manifestations. On the 11th November, Armistice Day, for example, a large crowd of some hundreds were shouting, singing and jeering at the Union Jack flying over The Bank of Ireland in College Green, Dublin, and also at the Loyalists waiting to observe the two minutes' silence. A tender of Auxiliaries drew up outside Trinity College, opposite the bank; the occupants dismounted, came smartly to attention and the crowd was immediately quietened and kept still. On the same day, Arthur Griffith wrote to the nine surviving hunger-strikers in Cork Gaol: 'I am of the opinion that our countrymen in Cork Prison have sufficiently proved their devotion, and that they should now, as they were prepared to die for Ireland, prepare again to live for her.' Two had already died. It was the ninety-fourth day of the fast and the end of hunger-striking in Ireland.

The I.R.A. in Dublin were under heavy pressure. Old soldiers, spoiling for a fight, liked to go down to the public houses on the quays and sing *God Save the King*. They were in search of trouble, but they seldom found it. The Intelligence Service in the Castle had been reorganised and raids became more frequent and more effective. British agents were trained in London and installed in Dublin under various innocent covers. They made their reports in a secret ink which, during the war, the Germans had never been able to develop. The offer of large rewards began to induce members of the lower ranks, and even some Commanders of the I.R.A., to impart information. The members of the I.R.A., from Michael Collins downwards, had a passion for committing plans to paper, and captured documents enabled the police to make many arrests and to forestall a number of attacks. In one such raid, papers belonging to Richard Mulcahy, the I.R.A.'s Chief of Staff, showed that a scientifically-minded Volunteer was thinking of earning the doubtful distinction of inventing bacteriological warfare. The papers suggested methods of infecting horses with glanders by doctoring their oats, and troops with typhoid by injecting the bacillus into their milk supply.

On the Irish side, Michael Collins had his own men in the detective division of the Dublin Metropolitan Police at the Castle, agents among some of the lower officials and secretaries there, and the help of a mysterious British intelligence officer who appears in his papers as Lt. G. Collins also organised raids for documents on the postal services, chiefly to trace informers and to mark them down for execution. The British authorities, however, used the mails very little by the autumn of 1920, as the Post Office was known to be thoroughly permeated with supporters of the I.R.A.

There was little that one side did not know about the

other, with the important qualification that the Castle authorities had the names of the men they wanted, but often no knowledge of what they looked like. Collins himself walked freely about Dublin, and men on the run were arrested, interrogated and released when they gave a convincing account of themselves. Collins believed, as he told an American reporter, that 'to paralyse the British machine it was necessary to strike at individuals. Without her spies England was helpless. It was only by their accumulated and accumulating knowledge that the British machine could operate.' He had accordingly removed the most dangerous members of the Detective Division of the Dublin Metropolitan Police by his campaign of selective assassination. But, by the late summer of 1920, he found that his campaign against the Castle Intelligence system had only scotched the snake. At first he underestimated the new threat to his security. Many of the new agents were identifiable by accent alone; some appeared content to draw their pay and do little for it. One, for example, lived at Vaughan's Hotel, which Collins used as a rendezvous with his staff; this agent often chatted with Collins and his companions but showed no interest in what they were doing or who they were— or so Collins at first supposed. 'Don't overdo,' Lt. G. warned him in a note. 'The road to Parnell Square is too well trod. Fifteen men, including you, went there to Vaughan's Hotel last night between 9 and 11 p.m.'

Murder took the place of battle throughout most of the Anglo-Irish war, a war in which both sides sought to eliminate wanted men. Many had prices on their heads from the £10,000 offered by the Castle for Michael Collins and Dan Breen, to the £50 Republican prize for a Black and Tan or an Auxiliary. A secret underground gang war developed in which fifteen murders were committed in July, eleven in August, eighteen in September, twenty in October and twenty-three in the first eighteen days of November. All of these were, at the time, attributed to the Crown Forces, and this charge was widely believed by liberal-minded people all over the world. It was not until the Civil War which broke out in the summer of 1922 after a minority in the Dáil had rejected the Anglo-Irish Treaty of 1921 that they saw the sadistic zest with which Irishmen could slaughter one another. For those who looked closely, this leopard already had its spots in 1920, and many of these murders were of Irishmen by Irishmen. Collins, like Lenin, believed that the purpose of terror is to terrify, and the members of his 'Squad' were not equipped with their Parabellums merely for ornament.

He had been convinced, after the killing of Lord Mayor MacCurtain in March, that a gang of counter-terrorists was at work, and that its members 'were going to put a lot of us on the spot'. He had decided to act first: throughout the summer his counter-intelligence had been shadowing suspects, intercepting letters and reports, eavesdropping, threatening violence and promising rewards. The trails they followed from Dublin Castle led all over the city, but many converged upon the Pembroke and Ballsbridge districts, where a group of English Secret Servicemen were living, ostensibly as ordinary civilians. It was not easy for them to be entirely secret; for one thing, they left their quarters at night, during the curfew hours, when no one but the Volunteers, the Crown Forces and drunks were abroad. They were known to their neighbours as 'hush-hush men', and were, naturally, the subject of excited speculation and local gossip. Their names and addresses were entered in the files hidden in the secret cupboard under the stairs in Collins' Intelligence Office in Mespil Road.

The murder of Mr. John Lynch in Vaughan's Hotel on the 23rd September, had given Collins another lead. This country business man was so unlikely to have started a gun battle with Intelligence officers, as the Castle statement had affirmed, that he decided to investigate the case and to exploit it for propaganda purposes. In the course of the

enquiry one of his agents tracked down the Secret Serviceman Anglis, alias MacMahon, one of the few English agents
able to pass himself off convincingly as an Irishman. After
the Lynch murder Anglis had taken to drink, and in a fit
of alcoholic frankness had spoken of his part in the affair
to a lady who could not keep a secret. Collins provided him
with drinking companions. An intercepted report also led
to a Captain Bagally, a court martial officer, who had only
participated in the raid to the extent of taking a telephone
message asking him to send a car to the R.I.C. depot. It
was not much, but it was enough to mark him down for
investigation and execution.

With the help of the mysterious English Intelligence
officer, Lt. G., Collins methodically collated his material
and, by the middle of November, was ready to act. On the
17th November he wrote to Dick McKee, Commander of
the Dublin Brigade: 'Dick—I have established the names
of the particular ones. Arrangements should now be made
about the matter. Lt. G. is aware of things. He suggests
the 21st. A most suitable date and day I think. M.' After
discussions with Cathal Brugha, the Minister of Defence,
and the Headquarters staff, Sunday, November the 21st,
to become known as 'Bloody Sunday', was confirmed as
the date. The plan was simple. Armed parties would make
simultaneous raids on all known Secret Service addresses
and kill as many agents as were at home. The battue would
be conducted by members of the Dublin Brigade with a
stiffening from the 'Squad' with their Parabellum and
Mauser automatics—'*my* Black and Tans', as Collins called
them.

On Saturday, the 20th, the eve of 'Bloody Sunday', a
group of the next day's executioners and some of their
victims were enjoying the play in adjacent rows at the
Gaiety Theatre. Collins was in the smoke room of Vaughan's
Hotel, checking the details of the Sunday morning programme with some of the staff of G.H.Q. and of the

Dublin Brigade, including Dick McKee and Peadar Clancy, its Brigadier and Vice-Brigadier. The meeting broke up and had not been long gone before a party of Auxiliaries burst into the smoking room with drawn guns. They had been well informed, but too late. They captured a Mr. Conor Clune, the head clerk of a firm in Raheer, County Clare, who had come up to Dublin with his employer on business, and bore this dangerous man in triumph to the Castle. At one o'clock in the morning, a Black and Tan raid in Lower Gloucester Street picked up Dick McKee and Peadar Clancy, who just had time to burn the list of officers to be shot and the orders of the day. It was an important capture, but the train for the explosion nine hours later had already been laid.

The church bells were ringing as eight groups of nervous assassins walked or bicycled through the quiet and almost empty streets to their assignment. It was a mild, sunny morning, twelve days after Lloyd George had assured the country that 'he had murder by the throat', and only two days after the ever-optimistic Sir Hamar Greenwood had told the House of Commons that 'things are very much better in Ireland'. As nine o'clock struck, a party of twenty men stopped outside No. 22 Lower Mount Street; their leader knocked on the door, which was opened by a maid. They rushed in, waving their revolvers and demanding to be shown the bedrooms occupied by MacMahon and Peel. One party burst into MacMahon's room and fired five shots at point-blank range, killing him in his bed. Others tried to break into Peel's room, but the door was locked. They fired seventeen wild shots through the door without hitting him.

The maid ran upstairs and leant out of a top-storey window, screaming for help. A platoon of Auxiliaries was passing on the way to the station to take train for the south; two men were sent back to the depot at Beggars Bush Barracks for reinforcements, while the rest broke into No. 22. The surprised Volunteers fled out of the back door,

[121]

through the garden and into a mews beyond. A long revolver shot winged one of them, Frank Teeling, and the Auxiliaries brought him back to the house.

The two Auxiliaries who had been sent back never reached the depot; a Volunteer picket on the canal bridge overpowered them, dragged them struggling into a back garden, and shot them against a wall. General Crozier was inspecting a newly-formed company of Auxiliaries at Beggars Bush Barracks before breakfast when he saw a military despatch rider on a motor bicycle, and a breathless Red Cross nurse on foot, approaching across the parade ground. They told him about the attack on the bridge. General Crozier raced to investigate with a platoon in Crossley tenders. He saw the maid leaning out of one of the top windows of No. 22 Lower Mount Street and heard her cries for help. He found one of his men holding a revolver at the head of the wounded Teeling and counting him out like a boxing referee; General Crozier knocked the pistol out of the Auxiliary's hand and had Teeling put into a tender to be taken to the George V Hospital as a prisoner awaiting trial.

He went upstairs to find the dead body of MacMahon, or Anglis, in one room, and Peel, an Irish Secret Serviceman, who had been saved by the arrival of the Auxiliaries, gibbering with panic in another. He left the house to look for his missing men. Their bodies were found in a neighbouring garden by the nurse who had seen them intercepted. They were the first Auxiliaries to be killed. Crozier, leaving his angry men to deal with their dead comrades, drove to Dublin Castle to report the three deaths.

He later described how he enjoyed shocking the 'superior intelligent crowd, mostly hoy hoy lah-di-dahs' in the mess and spoiling everyone's breakfast with his account of the morning's events. Then the telephone rang. The officer taking the call staggered, but steadied himself by holding on to the table.

'About fifty officers are shot,' he reported, 'in all parts of the city. Collins has done in most of the Secret Service people.'

The report was exaggerated, but the executioners had proceeded more or less according to plan and without the interruptions that had marred the operations at Lower Mount Street. While Crozier had been there, another armed party had already entered 38 Upper Mount Street, three hundred yards away. They asked the maid to show them the rooms occupied by Lieutenant Aimes, of the Grenadier Guards, and Lieutenant Bennett, of the Transport Corps. After showing them up, she rushed upstairs to warn another officer as well as a civilian male lodger. They heard a fusillade and came down to find that one officer had been dragged into the other's room. They were lying dead, side by side, in blood-soaked pyjamas.

At 28 Erlsfort Terrace the leader of the third armed band rang the bell and asked the maid for Colonel Fitzpatrick. There was no officer of that name in the house, but the maid obligingly indicated the room of a Captain Fitzgerald. The leader, a member of the 'Squad', called on his men and stationed them in the hall, then went up to Captain Fitzgerald's room. The maid heard the shouts of the victim, the executioner's curt command to 'Come on outa that', and then four shots in rapid succession. The police later found Fitzgerald's body in the blood-soaked bed, his forehead shattered by two bullets, another bullet through his wrist which he had thrown up in trying to protect himself, and a fourth through his heart. The aim had been more accurate than much of the shooting that morning. Captain Fitzgerald was a Tipperary man who had been acting as a defence officer of police barracks in County Clare. The local I.R.A. had already tried to kill him.

At No. 117 Morehampton Road, the ten-year-old son of Smith, the householder, opened the door. They pushed past him and ran up to the bedrooms. His mother and father were in bed in one room, and a Captain and Mrs. Maclean in another. He heard Captain Maclean begging them not to kill him in front of his wife. The Volunteers bundled Smith, Maclean and Mrs. Maclean's brother into an empty bedroom, but they were too nervous and appalled by the close-quarter carnage to shoot with accuracy. It is not everyone who enjoys killing unarmed men in cold blood, however noble they feel their cause to be. They ran out of the house, leaving all three men gravely wounded. Smith and Maclean were dead by the time the ambulance arrived but the other man recovered.

At the same time a party of about a dozen men knocked on the door of 92 Lower Bagot Street. When the landlady let them in, they asked for Captain Newbury, a court martial officer who lived there with his wife. They knocked at the bedroom door. Mrs. Newbury opened it, then, seeing armed men, quickly slammed and locked it. The Volunteers broke down the door; the couple had retreated to an inner room and tried to hold it against the assailants, but a shot through the door wounded Captain Newbury. He ran across the room and was half-way out of the window when the Volunteers burst in. Mrs. Newbury threw herself over her husband in an attempt to shield him. They dragged her away, then fired seven shots into his body. When help came, he was still half in and half out of the window, a blanket thrown over him by his distraught wife. She was pregnant and bore a still-born child a few days later.

There were no witnesses to the death of Captain Bagally, a few doors away, at No. 119. All the occupants of the house disappeared when the police arrived. The dead man had been a barrister by profession, had lost a leg in the war and had been a prosecutor under the Restoration of Order in Ireland Regulations. It was presumed that he had met his death in the same way as the rest. His room had been thoroughly searched.

The party of Volunteers that bicycled up to the block of

flats at 28 Upper Pembroke Street was better informed than the others. The men knew the house and where to find their objectives, without having to ask. Four Secret Service men lived in the house and the Volunteers killed two of them and fatally wounded a third; at the same time they seriously wounded three regimental officers. With the exception of two members of the 'Squad', the Volunteers were very nervous and the firing was wild.

An officer's wife has described the scene. The hall looked like a badly conducted abbattoir. Two dead Secret Servicemen and two badly wounded officers lay bleeding on the floor. Three of them had been playing cards with the American Consul until a late hour. The Consul had, fortunately, refused an invitation to stay the night and had thereby saved the Irish Republicans some diplomatic embarrassment. The walls were splashed with blood and sand poured from the bullet holes in the plaster. An old Irish lady with Sinn Fein sympathies was alarmed by the shooting and had a noisy fit of hysterics in her flat; she screamed curses at the British Government while an officer, who had been shot in the back, crawled past her door.

A Secret Serviceman had been dragged from a fourth-floor flat, struggling and shouting for help. He lay in blue pyjamas at the top of the kitchen stairs, shot through the lungs. A regimental officer who had come downstairs to see what was happening stood with his back to a wall while eight trembling Volunteers tried to take aim at him. They seemed sick with terror. This was not the way they had expected to fight for Ireland. One executioner's hand shook so badly that he was a danger to his comrades; the man on his right took his gun away from him. Even so, the officer who faced this firing squad was surprised to recover consciousness in hospital. Upstairs, the wife of an officer in the Lancashire Fusiliers wrestled with a group of Volunteers; as was to be seen later, there were killers in the I.R.A. who did not shrink from shooting women, but these young men were not made of such stern stuff. One of them managed to wound her husband in the shoulder as he ran to help her and then, having made the best of a bad job, the Volunteers fled down the stairs, out into the garden and through a gate unlocked for them by one of the servants.

The courage of the wives lent, in the opinion of Dubliners, at least some dignity to a shameful day. The I.R.A. later made as much propaganda as possible out of the disclosure that one of the victims had not been legally married to his lady. The seventh party, which entered the Gresham Hotel in Sackville Street and held up the head porter, differed from the others in that one member was armed with a sledge hammer. They asked for the rooms of Lieutenant Wilde and Captain McCormack, both of the Army Veterinary Service. A knock at No. 14 brought Wilde to the door to receive three shots in the chest. The door of No 22 was unlocked, and the Volunteers walked in to find McCormack sitting up in bed reading a newspaper; they fired five shots into his body and head. They later discovered that they had shot the wrong men.

* * * *

The entire I.R.A. campaign, carried out this Sunday morning, had been short and sharp, and by the time the ambulances, the police and military had arrived, the attackers had disappeared. Fourteen bodies, nine of them in pyjamas, were taken to the morgue; most of them had not been connected with either the Secret Service or Intelligence. 'Of course,' Collins explained to General Crozier after the truce, 'a few of your fellows, whom we didn't want to kill because we had nothing against them, walked on to the spot and had to be done in because they became dangerous evidence'. The wounded men were moved, some to a nursing home, some to a hospital. Guards were mounted over both buildings for, in an emotionally charged atmosphere, it seemed possible that the Volunteers might come back to finish the job.

The ebullient General Crozier, meanwhile, returned to Beggars Bush Barracks from the Castle; he completed his interrupted inspection and had breakfast. He, at least, was not overwhelmed by the general sense of horror; he played a game of squash, had a bath and then went to the Shelbourne Hotel to discuss the excitements of the morning over luncheon 'in the midst of cheery fellows, chaffing, laughing and speculating as to what the politicians would look like next day'.

But the next day was still some hours away. Crowds were converging on the Croke Park Sports Ground to watch a football game between Dublin and Tipperary; and it seemed probable that many of the gunmen would be attending the match. A plan was accordingly made to cordon off the ground with troops after the game had started, and to have the crowds systematically searched by police at the exits. So as to avert the danger of a stampede, an officer was to warn the crowd of what was to happen; but the company of Black and Tans from Phoenix Park, who were to carry out the search, arrived before this announcement had been made and were fired on by an I.R.A. picket patrolling the ground. The Black and Tans returned the fire. They killed one man walking with his fiancée, mortally wounded another and brought down a small boy who was sitting in a tree. A warning shot was fired from the crowd, and the Black and Tans began to shoot over the turnstiles. The intent and orderly spectators were at first stunned, and then broke into a cursing, screaming, frantic scramble of men, women and children. One player and eleven spectators were killed and many more injured in the stampede which made the search impossible, although thirty revolvers were found on the ground.

This massacre was not a reprisal for the murders of the morning as was claimed, but the unhappy product of

nervous strain and trigger-happy fingers. Nothing, however, could excuse the attack on the crowd, and it amply
redressed the day's balance of dishonour. There was an
explosive and ominous atmosphere in Dublin as darkness
fell. All trains out of the city were cancelled and outgoing
cars were searched. The trams were stopped and motor
traffic banned. Some irrational impulse kept Dubliners out
of doors until the curfew and the streets were crowded,
although it would have been far safer to stay indoors.
Military and police patrols were out in force, and in an
ugly, nervous mood. The explosion of bombs and the
crackle of shooting all over the city seemed to presage some
fearful disaster. Armoured cars and Crossley tenders, their
Black and Tan flags flying, rattled through the streets; at
their approach men and women threw up their hands and
ran distractedly about, like frightened hens, or fell on their
knees on the pavement.

Firing continued through the curfew hours. In Dublin
Castle, Irish officers of the Auxiliary Company, known to
the I.R.A. as 'the Dublin Castle murder gang', crowned an
inglorious day by killing Dick McKee, Peadar Clancy and
the clerk Conor Clune. The Castle Press office later issued
an account of how the prisoners had tried to fight their way
out with grenades. Sir John Anderson was by no means the
only person to suspect the truth of this story, but he was
able to investigate all the circumstances and assure the
Government that on this occasion, at least, the official
version was substantially correct. Nothing in his record,
either then or later, suggested that he was a man to condone
unnecessary violence. But the case of the non-combatant,
Clune, whose republicanism was limited to an interest in
Gaelic literature, could not be explained away, and he had
to be posthumously promoted, in the Castle report, and
given a lieutenancy in the 1st Battalion Clare Brigade,
I.R.A.

The death roll of 'Bloody Sunday' was complete. The

30. Crown Forces: An unarmed constable of the Dublin Metropolitan Police stands between two Auxiliaries. A soldier and a plain clothes man greeting a Black and Tan complete the picture.

31. Ministers and their agents: Lloyd George receives men of the Royal Irish Constabulary and reviews a parade of Auxiliaries in Downing Street. With him are Sir Hamar Greenwood and Mr. Bonar Law.

32. A group of Dublin Castle Intelligence Officers known to the Volunteers as 'the Murder Gang': This photograph, taken in Lower Castle Yard, fell into the hands of the I.R.A. The numbers refer to the names on the back, where Nos. 1, 2 and 3 are marked as being Irish.

33. Barricades and barbed wire entanglements make Dublin Castle almost a beleaguered fortress. Officials are unable to stir abroad without an armed escort.

murders caused a temporary revulsion against the I.R.A. Cardinal Logue and the Archbishop of Dublin both expressed their detestation of the battue, but this feeling was not shared by at least one churchman, and Father Dominic, who had attended Terence MacSwiney during his hunger strike in Brixton Gaol, wrote from Cork: 'What a glorious day for Ireland was Sunday 21st November. Down here for our part we have not been idle; we captured six officers, and they squealed like rats before they went on their way to light and glory.' He later agreed, when he was arrested, that these were scarcely Christian sentiments.

In London, the politicians were not as disconcerted as General Crozier and his cheery companions in the Shelbourne Hotel had hoped. Sir Henry Wilson was enraged by what seemed to him to be the callous indifference of the Cabinet, or 'the frocks', as he called them. He let himself go in his diary: 'Tonight Winston insinuated that the murdered officers were careless, and ought to have taken precautions. This fairly roused me, and I let fly about the Cabinet being cowards and not governing, but leaving it to the "Black and Tans", etc. No Cabinet meeting, as the Cabinet do not think that anything out of the way has happened! I urged on Winston, for the hundredth time, that the Government should govern, should proclaim their fidelity to the Union, and declare Martial Law. I told him I had not intended to speak on Ireland, as it was useless. But I was angry at the Ministerial attitude about these poor wounded officers, and I frightened Winston.' Sir Henry was the first, but not the last, C.I.G.S. to have trouble with Winston Churchill.

'Bloody Sunday' was over. All that now remained was to bury the dead and find the culprits. On the following Thursday, the 25th November, six of the military victims were given a State Funeral in Westminster Abbey. Lloyd George, Winston Churchill and Hamar Greenwood walked up the aisle behind the coffins. Sir Henry Wilson wondered why they did not hide their heads in shame. He contrasted the ceremony unfavourably with the interment of the Unknown Soldier a few days earlier.

In Ireland five hundred Sinn Feiners had been arrested in all parts of the country within forty-eight hours, on information supplied by General Tudor's Intelligence Service. Among them were William O'Brien, Thomas Faron and Thomas Johnson, all of the Irish Trade Union Congress and Labour Party. The Castle authorities produced another form to put in the file, and witnesses were asked to answer such questions as 'How many murders were committed in your presence?' and 'Were the murderers armed?' The witnesses were also taken for a tour of the prisons, where they were made to stand in specially constructed huts to look through slits cut in felt curtains which allowed them to see without being seen. The prisoners were paraded in front of them in batches of ten, and young Smith was certain that he could recognise 'the men who killed Daddy'.

Collins made all the arrangements for the funeral of McKee and Clancy, the only I.R.A. casualties of 'Bloody Sunday'. He felt their loss keenly, and was one of the twenty worshippers to take the risk of attending the Requiem Mass for their souls. Two men were later executed for taking part in the 'Bloody Sunday' battue. Teeling, the only I.R.A. prisoner to be taken that day, escaped from Kilmainham gaol with the help of a corrupt British soldier, to continue a meaningless life of violence and homicide. Like many, but not all of the gunmen, he was probably what would now be recognised as an aggressive psychopath. Of all the participants in the events of 'Bloody Sunday', he, at least, found his true home in a mental institution.

CHAPTER NINE

Peace Moves and Arson

THE EVENTS of 'Bloody Sunday' exposed the practical and moral bankruptcy of both sides. 'Murder begets murder,' *The Daily Mail* commented. 'Yesterday's slaughter is the dreadful result of a policy of illegal violence to which the Government has for months turned a blind eye.' Lord Grey told the House of Lords: 'Ireland is a greater obstacle to international goodwill than any other question.' The British Anglican Bishops urged 'that military terrorism may cease and a truce be arranged.' The Peace with Ireland Council held a mass meeting at the Albert Hall, under the chairmanship of Lord Henry Cavendish-Bentinck, at which members of all parties and a number of churchmen condemned both murders and reprisals. 'What I want to know,' said Miss Margaret Bondfield, the woman Labour leader, 'is which are the reprisals and which are the murders?' Shortly after the meeting, General Sir Henry Lawson went to Ireland on a fact-finding mission, as an envoy of the Council. The Labour Party also appointed a commission to investigate conditions in Ireland. An Anti-Reprisal Association had been formed, and both Mrs. Despard, the Viceroy's sister, and Archbishop Mannix were addressing meetings up and down the country on Ireland's claim to self-determination. Lloyd George was under attack from all sides. He was anxious to negotiate a settlement, but was not prepared to surrender.

There was still no room for manoeuvre, but many Sinn Feiners were ready to break the deadlock caused by the Dáil's intransigent demand for an independent Republic.

On the 20th October a Conservative Member of Parliament Brigadier-General George Cockerill, had written a letter to *The Times* proposing a truce and a peace conference, and Arthur Griffith had approved this proposal in an interview. In the middle of November, a well-known American journalist, John S. Steele, appointed himself peace-maker; both he and Mr. P. Moylett, a Dublin business man with Sinn Fein sympathies, came to London with a written confirmation of Arthur Griffith's approval of General Cockerill's plan. They discussed it with members of Lloyd George's staff. Lloyd George said he was interested and asked Steele and Moylett to act as intermediaries with the Republican leaders. On the 24th November a venerable Sinn Fein figure, George Russell, an economist who was also the poet A.E., came to London to explore the possibilities of a peaceful settlement in a conversation with Lloyd George. On the same day Arthur Griffith was arrested in Dublin and the Prime Minister, very angry to learn of the arrest told the astonished General Macready, who did not know of the peace negotiations, that he had no right to take such an action without the sanction of the Cabinet.

Peace was in the air, but violence was still in full stride. On the 27th November the I.R.A. brought their war across the sea, and Volunteers in Liverpool set fire to fifteen cotton warehouses and timber yards; another plot to fire a timber yard in Aldersgate, London, was betrayed by an informer. Barriers were erected across the approaches to Downing Street; the public galleries were closed in the House of Commons and in the House of Lords: Scotland Yard was ordered to provide police protection to Sir Henry Wilson, who wrote in his diary: 'We must stamp out these murderous pests or we shall be ruined. Two of these 'murderous pests' later assassinated Sir Henry Wilson outside his house in Eaton Place in June, 1922. On the same day, General Crozier was investigating the murder of a priest by a party of Auxiliaries in Galway, and discovered a plot to murder

Bishop Fogarty of Killaloe; the Bishop's body was to be thrown in a weighted sack into the River Shannon. Dr. Fogarty was, unlike most of the Hierarchy, a staunch Republican, and was one of the trustees of the Dáil loan. He had declared, as early as 1919, that: 'The fight for Irish freedom has passed into the hands of the young men of Ireland . . . and when the young men of Ireland hit back, it is not for an old man like me to cry "Foul".' This spirited cleric was not at home when the Auxiliaries called for him On the next day, the 28th November, a Flying Column of the Third Cork Brigade ambushed an Auxiliary patrol of eighteen men in two tenders from Macroom. They killed seventeen, savagely mutilated their bodies after death, and left one man, with several bullet wounds and an axe wound in his head, for dead. One man was missing, and his body was never found. Three Volunteers were killed, an unusually high casualty rate for an operation of this kind. The Macroom ambush, as it became known, had a heartening effect on the I.R.A. For three months the Auxiliaries had been raiding, searching and patrolling the district without being attacked; they had rounded-up suspects and had frequently added physical injury to insults. In Ireland, where legends grow quickly, they had, even in this short time, acquired the reputation of being, in the words of an I.R.A. commander, 'super-fighters and all but invincible'. So notable a victory was, accordingly, celebrated in a ballad, which made the common mistake of confusing the Auxiliaries with the Black and Tans:

> On the twenty-eighth day of November just outside the town of Macroom
> The Tans in their big Crossley tenders, they hurried along to their doom
> For the boys of the Column were waiting with hand grenades pinned on the spot
> And the Irish Republican Army made shit of the whole f***ing lot.

The attack was followed by the usual outbreak of arson; a number of farm houses and barns were burned in the area of the ambush and many buildings in Cork went up in flames on the following days. Fire-brigades refused to move without military escort, and the Unionist Association sent a telegram to the Government demanding both an enquiry and immediate protection for citizens' property. In the course of these reprisals a party of drunken Black and Tans struck down an ex-British officer as he was leaving the Royal Hotel in Fermoy; they killed him by throwing him over the parapet into the River Blackwater, which was in spate. They followed up this act of senseless savagery by breaking into the house next to the hotel, dragging a man out of bed and hurling him too into the river. They then set the house on fire, and when the military arrived to quench the flames, cut the hoses and left the scene. A few days later, the Auxiliary Division of the Royal Irish Constabulary, stationed at Macroom Castle, issued the following proclamation, to be posted up, and also printed in the local Press:

Whereas foul murders of servants of the Crown have been carried out by disaffected persons, and whereas such persons, immediately before the murders, appeared to be peaceful and loyal people, but have produced pistols from their pockets, therefore it is ordered that all male inhabitants of Macroom and all males passing through Macroom shall not appear in public with their hands in their pockets. Any male infringing this order is liable to be shot at sight.

These events, and the almost daily round of murder and reprisal, terror and counter-terror, were enacted under the spot-light of newspaper publicity that suggested that the whole of Ireland was racked with disorder and aflame with military activity. But in thirteen of the Twenty-six Counties there had been no I.R.A. activity during the month of

November, and the Volunteers' war effort was, as before, almost entirely concentrated in Dublin and in the South and West. A number of faint-hearts had left the ranks under the combined pressure of the Black and Tans and the Restoration of Order in Ireland Act. In the three months, between the beginning of September and the end of November, five hundred and sixty-six Irishmen had been tried by court martial under the Act, and three hundred convicted. In addition to specific charges, that of 'being suspected of acting, having acted, and being about to act in a manner prejudicial to the maintenance and restoration of order in Ireland,' was sufficiently wide to include almost everyone. The number of I.R.A. operations, including raids for arms, raids on the mails, attacks on barracks, coastguard stations, policemen and soldiers, had declined from a total of over two thousand in September to less than three hundred in November. Few Irishmen were prepared to fight though many would sing, with all their hearts, the curious ditty which ran:

Up de Valera, the hero of the right.
We'll follow him to battle with orange green and white.
We'll beat old England well and give her hell's delight.
Up de Valera, King of Ireland!

Whatever their feelings about England, the majority of Irish people were tired of the war, and a proposal for an immediate conference, to stop the bloodshed, made by Roger Sweetman, a member of the Dáil, in a letter to the Press on the 30th November, was greeted with an enthusiasm which alarmed the diehards of the I.R.A. 'If only the people in England knew,' a special correspondent of *The Times* wrote of the general war weariness and desire for peace. 'Everywhere in Ireland you hear that cry. Men and women of every shade of political opinion and religious faith—Catholics, Protestants, Unionists, Nationalists, even large numbers of Sinn Feiners, are united in that inarticulate appeal.'

[135]

In London another mediator appeared on the political scene in the person of The Most Reverend Dr. Clune, Archbishop of Perth, Western Australia, who was also an uncle of Conor Clune who had been killed in Dublin Castle on the night of 'Bloody Sunday'. He had an interview with Lloyd George and was empowered, by him, to go to Dublin to discuss proposals for a truce with Arthur Griffith, who was in gaol, and with Michael Collins, who was wanted by the police, alive or dead. In a reply to a question in the House of Commons about peace with Ireland, Lloyd George said: 'I shall not wait until the approach of Christmas to take any possible steps to secure that object.' Dr. Clune went at once to Dublin and saw Arthur Griffith who sent him to the Secretary of the Dáil with this letter:

> Archbishop Clune will show you a letter he brought to me from London. It should go on to the Minister of Finance and the Ministry generally.
> It would be indiscreet for the Archbishop to see M.C., although they have guaranteed that he will not be subject to espionage. We cannot trust them, but through you communications will be established, or through some other person whom you point out to His Grace.
> The Labour Leaders, Henderson and Adamson, were here yesterday. I referred them to what I stated in public to Brigadier Cockerill's proposals. They are anxious for a truce, and a meeting with Dáil Eireann.
> The proposals for a truce the Archbishop conveys involve no surrender of principle on our part, I believe. If the English Government calls off its present aggressive campaign, we can respond by urging the cessation of the present acts of self-defence. All the pursuit of Members of the Dáil and others must cease, and the entire Dáil freely meet to arrange the full terms of the truce.

Excited rumours of immediate peace swept over Ireland.

On the 3rd December the Galway County Council passed a resolution deploring both the I.R.A.'s campaign and the reprisals by the Crown Forces. It called upon the Dáil to appoint three delegates 'who will have power to arrange a truce and preliminary terms of a peace honourable to both countries'. On the next day, Michael Collins walked through the streets of Dublin, with a £10,000 price on his head and a folded newspaper under his arm as a means of recognition, to meet Archbishop Clune, the emissary of the British Government. They agreed on a formula for a truce, afterwards confirmed by Michael Collins in the following letter:

> If it is understood that the acts of violence (attacks, counter-attacks, reprisals, arrests, pursuits) are called off on both sides, we are agreeable to issue the necessary instructions on our side, it being understood that the entire Dáil shall be free to meet, and that its peaceful activities be not interfered with.

Father O'Flanagan, the Acting President of Sinn Fein, had also visited London with the Lord Justice O'Connor in a private attempt to negotiate peace; on his return to Ireland, he sent a telegram to Lloyd George: 'You state that you are willing to make peace at once without waiting for Christmas. Ireland also is willing. What first steps do you propose?'

The war parties on both sides were disturbed by these peace moves. In Ireland, Michael Collins was anxious for a truce, but suspicious of Saxon treachery, as he showed in a statement to the Press: 'At the present moment there is very grave danger that the country may be stampeded on false promises and foolish ill-timed actions. We must stand up against that danger. My advice to the people is to "hold fast".' He also wrote a letter to *The Irish Independent* which the paper dared not publish: 'Now is the time to ensure that what the enemy has not been able to do by force or fraud or political wile, he shall not do by propagandist jugglery of the pleasant peace-talk variety. Wait for the fulfilment of the promises. Meanwhile, get on with the work.' In London, Sir Henry Wilson pressed for the imposition of martial law on the whole of Ireland. He had won Winston Churchill, the Secretary for War, to this opinion, but Lloyd George, who awaited the return of Archbishop Clune, would not agree; he compromised by telling Sir Henry that he was in favour of starting martial law in Cork, Kerry and Limerick and that it could be extended later. Sir Hamar Greenwood, who had come back from Ireland with the report that the I.R.A. was 'on the run everywhere', thought martial law unnecessary.

This estimate was supported by a report received at the War Office of a conversation between the American Consul and General Boyd, the Commander of the British troops in Dublin. The Consul said that he had information that the I.R.A. wanted to get in touch with the British Army, with a view to arranging terms of peace; he told the General that he could introduce him to a Sinn Feiner 'who was not one of the murder gang'. A meeting was arranged, and this self-appointed spokesman, who claimed to speak for the I.R.A., including Michael Collins, reported that the Volunteers had no faith in either their own politicians or in Lloyd George, and that they wanted to come to an arrangement with the military. Sir Henry Wilson was greatly heartened by this report and other symptoms in Ireland of a desire for peace. 'Macready, Boyd and I had a long discussion and were agreed that it was out of the question to hold parley with the rebel murderers,' he wrote in his diary on the 7th December, 'and the thing to do was to clap on martial law at once, as it was evident that the murderers were getting rattled.'

Archbishop Clune returned to London on the 8th December, and had another interview with Lloyd George, whom he found to be anxious for peace; but, at the same time, he gave the impression of being under pressure from his military advisers to adopt a tough policy. While the

Archbishop was still with him, Lloyd George summoned
a meeting of the Cabinet, which was also attended by
General Macready and Sir John Anderson. After a lengthy
discussion the war party gained the ascendancy, and the
Cabinet agreed to impose martial law on Cork, Kerry,
Limerick and Tipperary. General Macready told Sir Henry
Wilson that it was not to be put into effect for a fortnight,
so that an appeal could first be made to the priests to urge
the rebels to surrender their arms. 'At long last,' Sir Henry
Wilson wrote in his diary, 'it is a beginning of the Government governing.' In announcing the partial imposition of
martial law to the House of Commons two days later,
Lloyd George said: 'We could not recognise Dáil Eireann.
The section which controls the organisation of violence,
murder and outrage is not yet ready to negotiate a peace
which will accept the only basis on which a peace can be
concluded—the acceptance of the unbroken unity of the
United Kingdom. We are determined to break up these
terrorists.' At the same time, he asked Dr. Clune to return
to Ireland to continue negotiations.

Meanwhile, the Volunteers were obeying Michael
Collins' unpublished injunction 'to get on with the work'.
Cork had been the centre of terror and counter-terror since
the Macroom ambush, and on the 11th December another
ambush party successfully attacked an Auxiliary patrol with
grenades and revolver fire at Dillon's Cross, about two
hundred yards from the military barracks in the city; they
killed one Auxiliary and wounded eleven. The news of
this attack spread terror through the city of Cork. At nine
o'clock, Auxiliaries stopped the trams in Patrick Street,
forced the passengers to alight and then stand to be searched,
their hands above their heads. Several men were beaten
up, including a priest who had very naturally refused to
say 'to hell with the Pope'. Half an hour before curfew, the
streets were deserted. At about ten o'clock, Auxiliaries and
Black and Tans set fire to two houses near Dillon's Cross

[139]

and prevented attempts to extinguish the flames. At the same time Auxiliaries and Black and Tans began crowding the streets, shooting into the air and yelling. Flames soon reddened the sky above the city as the central shopping district was systematically looted and destroyed by bombs and by arson. By midnight columns of black smoke, shot with flames, rose from the blazing buildings. Many of the Auxiliaries and Black and Tans were drunk and were shooting wildly, to the great danger of the fire-brigade. One detachment of firemen urged a party of Black and Tans to cut their hoses so that they could go home, but on many occasions the incendiarists performed this service without having to be asked. In a night of frenzied disorder, soldiers, and even some Auxiliaries and Black and Tans, tried to fight the fires while others extended them.

As the night advanced, civilians, who were driven from their homes by fear of the encroaching flames, began to appear on the streets, and Volunteers joined the soldiers and police who were fighting the fires. A resolute band of Cork women joined in the looting of a drapery store; a merry group of drunken Black and Tans cavorted, singing and dancing through the streets with a bevy of Irish girls who had, in the general excitement, forgotten about the boycott of the police, and Auxiliaries were treating the ladies of the town to looted drinks in back parlours. Uniformed figures were to be seen everywhere, staggering through the fire-lit streets, with valises bulging with loot. At two o'clock in the morning the incendiary forces of law and order broke into both the City Hall and Carnegie Library and by four o'clock, after one unsuccessful attempt, had them both blazing well with the use of bombs and petrol. A party of police guarded the hydrants and turned off the water every time the firemen turned it on. By five, the clock tower of the City Hall was glowing as though it were floodlit and the clock went on striking the hour until six-fifteen, when it crashed into the ruins below.

Few worshippers ventured out when the church bells rang for mass. The police had withdrawn at about five o'clock, but military patrols were still on the streets; some of them were also the worse for drink. As it became light, hundreds came out to see the damage: Patrick Street, the main street of the city, had been laid waste; twenty-one shops had been completely destroyed. In all, forty shops had been burned to the ground, twenty-four partially damaged and many more looted. The damage was estimated at £3 million, but only two deaths were recorded. At two in the morning a party of Black and Tans had raided a farm just outside the city which had been used as an I.R.A. arms and ammunition store; they killed two sons of the house who were active Volunteers, and this, in the opinion of one historian of the I.R.A., was 'the most ghastly deed of all that night of horror', though whether it was worse than any of the other murders committed by either side is open to question. Over thirty years later an old and unrepentant Black and Tan, by that time dressed in the respected uniform of a Chelsea Pensioner, was asked to account for the behaviour of the Crown Forces on that night. 'Well you see,' he said after a moment's reflection, 'it was near Christmas.'

Dr. Cohalan, Bishop of Cork, was among those who considered murder to be murder by whomsoever committed, and in a pastoral letter read in the churches of his diocese the night after the fires, condemned reprisals and the oppression of the Crown Forces and launched the sentence of excommunication against the murderers of policemen and others. 'The killing of police is morally murder and politically of no consequence,' he declared, 'and the burning of barracks is simply the destruction of Irish property.' The citizens of Cork were more urgently concerned with the destruction of Irish property by the Crown Forces; there was an immediate demand for an impartial civilian enquiry into the events of this night of arson, both by Sinn Fein and Unionist organisations.

In the House of Commons Sir Hamar Greenwood protested most vigorously against the suggestion that these fires were started by the police or by the troops. He contended that 'the Forces of the Crown had saved Cork from destruction'. Who started the fires? He pointed out that most of the destroyed property did not belong to members to members of Sinn Fein and invited the House to draw its own conclusions. 'It is obvious,' he said, 'that a fire of this kind is the only possible argument that is used against the Government policy in Ireland.' He argued, in a most unfortunate passage, that the City Hall and the Carnegie Library had not been deliberately burned, but that the fire had spread to these buildings from Patrick Street. To do that the flames would have had to leap a quarter of a mile over a number of unburned streets and across the River Lee. He had been badly briefed, but, none the less, this lamentable defence of the indefensible did more than anything else to discredit him and the Liberal Party to which he belonged. The Liberals in the Cabinet detested what was being done and kept silent; they held on to office when they might, more honourably and sensibly, have joined their old leader, Mr. Asquith, and the twenty-five other Independent Liberals on the Opposition benches. The Liberal Party did not perish in the fires of Cork, but its structure and support was seriously damaged.

The official suggestion that Cork had been burned by its own citizens was a surprise even to the Auxiliaries, a party of whom further discredited the force by holding up and threatening to shoot the members of the Labour Party Commission who came to investigate. Even without this encouragement, the Commission told the Prime Minister in a telegram that it was 'convinced that the fires were the work of the Crown Forces', and offered to produce 'reliable evidence on the subject'. The Cork Incorporated Chamber of Commerce and Shipping, a predominantly Unionist body, sent a telegram to Sir Hamar Greenwood expressing their 'astonishment at the statement made by you in the House of Commons with reference to the destruction of Cork', and demanded that a Judicial Commission of Enquiry should be set up and that all damage should be made good out of public funds.

The Government resisted the pressure to set up an independent enquiry, and, on the 16th December, General Strickland, the Commanding Officer in Cork, opened a military enquiry. Maurice Healy, an ex-M.P. for Cork and a solicitor, applied formally, on behalf of the Cork Incorporated Chamber of Commerce and Shipping and the Cork Employers' Federation, to be allowed to be present and to give evidence. He was told that lawyers would not be admitted. He wrote for written confirmation of this refusal on the 17th December, and again on the 21st, when he received a communication from General Strickland which read: 'As the court of inquiry has now closed, your question does not arise.' The citizens of Cork were quick to observe that the inquiry had closed before ever it was opened. The Strickland report was never published, mistakenly in the opinion of General Macready, because, as he later wrote, 'it gave greater scope to rebel propaganda, and it was no secret in the town as to who were the culprits'. In spite of the official secrecy, it was known, both in Dublin Castle and outside, that the report placed the chief responsibility for the arson and looting on a company of Auxiliaries who had recently been sent to Cork. This company was withdrawn to Dublin, where they tactlessly wore burnt corks in their glengarries as a defiant memento of their riotous night out. Their commanding officer returned to England and, a few weeks later, shot himself on Wimbledon Common.

Meanwhile, the peace negotiations continued. Dr. Clune and Dr. Fogarty saw Arthur Griffith in gaol, and the Cabinet sent him a message through Sir John Anderson. It asked that there should be no public functioning of the Dáil during the truce. Throughout these negotiations,

Arthur Griffith was in constant communication with Michael Collins, who had his agents in Mountjoy Gaol, as elsewhere. Reporting on the Cabinet proposals, he wrote to Collins: 'One of the most important members summed up the situation in a sentence. "Ask your fellows to lie low for a month or so. Then the atmosphere and temper over there will be different." I sincerely believe the Premier is genuinely anxious to bring about peace, but he had great difficulties. The Cork burnings have strengthened his hands against his Diehards.' Collins was not convinced that Lloyd George wanted peace and wrote, strangely: 'I don't think such a consideration matters.' He was not distinguished for his political sense, and thought at first that 'it would be fatal to have any proposal for settlement with England without a reparation clause'. But by the 15th December the two sides seemed very close to agreement.

Griffith was politically more adroit and it is possible that his partly Welsh temperament gave him a closer insight into Lloyd George's motives. He thought 'the truce in the terms we outlined will be of advantage to the country. They are fighting their Diehard militarists, and the truce on such terms would assist them.' But on the next day, Dublin Castle only agreed to a truce, subject to the important proviso that the Volunteers surrendered their arms. Arthur Griffith told Dr. Clune that there could be no surrender under any circumstances and again wrote to Michael Collins secretly from gaol: 'He believes the reply comes from Greenwood and Co. rather than Lloyd George. He goes to London tonight to see Lloyd George and will tell him if surrender of arms is insisted upon, all is off.' Before returning to London, Dr. Clune had a short meeting with Collins, who agreed that the demand for the surrender of arms meant the end of negotiations, and an interview with Sir John Anderson who said he was prepared to waive this condition. So, by the time Dr. Clune reached London, were Lloyd George and Bonar Law. He was asked to hold

34. Lord French reviews a parade of Auxiliaries at their depot in Phoenix Park. He is followed (centre) by General Tudor, who commands and has reorganised and re-equipped the police for offensive action.

35. A famous I.R.A. Flying Column in Mayo: These men 'defied six hundred British troops at Tour-makeady' according to *An t-Oglach*. They lost one man and six shotguns in this famous battle.

36. Five hundred arrests were made within forty-eight hours of the murders of 'Bloody Sunday', 21st November, 1920. An Auxiliary Cadet has picked up a couple of suspects in the Ministry of Labour Offices in the Rotunda, Dublin, and marches them through the streets at the pistol point.

37. *An t-Oglach* was distributed weekly to all units of the I.R.A. It was delivered hidden in flour sacks, furniture packing cases and many other disguises. It mixed encouragement with practical advice, and often had to make up with fighting words for a lack of activity in the field.

An t-Óglác

THE OFFICIAL ORGAN OF THE IRISH VOLUNTEERS.

Vol. IV. No. 9.]   MAY 20, 1921.   [Price Twopence.

"GET ON WITH THE WAR"

The soldiers of the Irish Republican Army have every reason to be satisfied with the progresss of the War of Independence. At no previous period have we been in a stronger position; at no time were our prospects brighter. The wonderful development of fighting efficiency in our army has opened up immensely greater possibilities than were realised in the earlier stages of the campaign; and the enemy after six months of the most strenuous exertion in which every device of civilised and uncivilised warfare has been resorted to against us finds himself baffled, further than ever from any encouraging tokens of success, in a worse military position than ever before. His "frightfulness" has done useful service to us in putting Volunteers on their mettle and giving them an additional incentive to waging war more strenuously against us. The offensive remains with us and it is going to remain. In the immediate future the enemy may expect a big

in his professed desire for peace he can have it in 24 hours simply by stopping his aggression. All he has to do is to remove his army of occupation, and peace will reign throughout the land. He knows in his heart he will have to do it some day if he cannot succeed in entangling our Government in "negotations" involving a "compromise." He will not succeed. There will be no compromise. The Republic of Ireland IS and WILL BE. The orders from our Government are: Get on with the War. It is our business to wage war on the foreign aggressor with every scrap of energy at our disposal. We are waging a great and holy fight for our country's freedom; we have won wonderful victories; and are militarily in a stronger position than ever before. The Army of the Irish Republic and the people of Ireland generally have made great sacrifices and sustained much suffering with splendid fortitude and unbroken spirit. They have nothing worse to dread in the future than what they himself in readiness for another journey to Ireland, but the call never came. The war party in Dublin Castle and the divded Cabinet had momentarily won the day and by devious means, which included the circulation of an intelligence report that Michael Collins was opposed to the truce and would not observe it.

By inserting the condition that arms should be surrendered, the war party in the Cabinet hoped either to achieve a victory or to demonstrate that Ireland was not subject to its elected government, but to the gunmen. Certainly, Michael Collins could no more have disarmed the I.R.A. in 1920, even if he had wanted to, than he could in 1922 when he made the attempt. Ambushes and reprisals, meanwhile, had continued throughout the peace negotiations. Seven members of the R.I.C. and two soldiers were killed and six R.I.C. and ten soldiers wounded during the week ending the 20th December. On the 15th December an Auxiliary, recovering from the effects of delirium tremens, shot an old priest and a young man in Cork, without provocation of any kind, thereby causing yet another scandal and further angry exchanges in the House of Commons. This criminal was later tried for murder and found guilty but insane. The Auxiliaries had by this time become so notorious that Sir John Anderson advocated disbanding them. General Macready was opposed to any weakening of the police and military forces, and observed, justly enough, that the excesses of a few should not be a reason for condemning the Auxiliary Division as a whole. Most of the Auxiliary companies were feared and respected as formidable and disciplined fighters.

Martial law, in force in the four Southern counties, created as many difficulties as it solved. The patrolling of the border-lines between martial law and civil law areas made a heavy call on troops. In the area of one military division, half the population might be under martial law and half under civil, with the result that a man could, theoretically, be sentenced to death in one place while another, within a few hundred yards, would receive a maximum sentence of two years' hard labour for the same offence. In a letter from London to his second in command, General Macready, after a meeting with Lloyd George, reported that the Prime Minister had told him 'he was most anxious that, while we put the screws on the rebels to the greatest degree, we and the police should rather go out of our way not to be disagreeable to the unoffending inhabitants'. Macready observed that it was difficult to distinguish between the offending and unoffending. It seemed to him that the Prime Minister was trying to repress outrage with one hand, while waving an olive branch with the other. 'So it will be up to us,' he concluded, 'to try and play up to what seems to be a somewhat complicated policy.'

It was, as the event was to show, a wise and successful policy. Lloyd George was never impressed with the military effort of the Irish Republican Army which the soldiers so often exaggerated to excuse their own lack of success. He resolutely refused to let them have the powers demanded by Sir Henry Wilson, powers which were so effectively used many years later in one way by the Nazis in occupied Europe, and in another by the British in Kenya. There were no mass executions of either prisoners or hostages—'shooting by roster' as Sir Henry Wilson called it—and no vast inhuman concentration camps in Ireland. The Sinn Fein propagandists, however, made as much as they could of 'the horror of the prison camps' in which the men convicted at court martials were interned. But letters from the victims contained such phrases as: 'Our drill is improving every day; we shall be a crack company when we get out', and 'Tell Mother we get plenty of spuds to our dinner and plenty of beef too, so we don't want anything except for an odd cake for supper as we only get three meals a day'. Conditions were not, it seems, too oppressive.

Under the martial law ordinances, which were based on those issued in the Boer War, the offences for which the death sentence could be imposed included the possession of arms, ammunition or explosives, the wearing of Irish Volunteer uniform and harbouring, aiding or abetting rebels. General Macready issued a martial law circular warning all members of the Crown Forces that offences against civilians and the plundering of houses were also liable to punishment by death. Official reprisals and punishments by confiscation, fines and the destruction of houses by explosive also came into force in the martial law areas. This power was used sparingly, and the destruction conducted in an orderly and humane manner, with the passage of the appropriate documents, the orders passing from in-trays to out-trays and the full reports and returns of military bureaucratic procedure. These official reprisals provided fresh ammunition for the opponents of the Government in spite of, or perhaps because of, their official character. A system of military permits for all motor cars was also introduced in an attempt to deny the use of motor transport to the Volunteers. The riding of bicycles was also prohibited in areas in which ambushes had been laid.

With or without a permit, the hard-pressed Irish motorist was liable to have his car commandeered by the military on Monday, by the Royal Irish Constabulary on Tuesday, the Auxiliaries on Wednesday, the I.R.A. on Thursday and a band of armed robbers on Friday, leaving him the week-end in which to trace and, with luck, recover it, and have it ditched on the way home in a trench dug in the road by the Volunteers, or blocked by felled trees or loose stone walls. These obstacles frequently provided the occasion for an ambush, and were designed to combat the growing mobility of the Crown Forces, and reduce the effectiveness of the Peerless and Rolls-Royce armoured cars, which began to make their appearance on the roads in the South and

West, and undermine the morale of the fainter-hearted Volunteers.

The leaders of the I.R.A. could, and did, make confident statements. 'Let Lloyd George make no mistake,' Michael Collins wrote during the truce negotiations of mid-December, 'the I.R.A. is not broken. The events of the week and these days are more eloquent on that question than all his military advisers. Neither is the spirit of the people subdued . . .' The I.R.A. was certainly not broken, but it was being contained. The number of operations of all kinds conducted by the Volunteers in December dropped below even November's low level, and in most parts of the country the I.R.A. still existed in name alone. Merchants and farmers who had prospered in the Great War feared the approach of ruin in this lesser one. Unemployment was widespread and Marxism seemed to many of the workless a surer guide to an earthly paradise than Sinn Fein. The law-abiding population, the great majority of the people of Ireland, wished bad cess to Volunteer and Black and Tan alike. On the 14th December the National Executive of the Irish Trade Union Congress and Labour Party ended the seven months' resistance of the railway and dockworkers and advised them 'to offer to carry everything that the British authorities are prepared to risk on the trains'. The Executive of the National Union of Railwaymen in London had refused, throughout, to authorise the action of the Irish workers, partly through an ingrained reluctance to commit itself to any definite course of action, and partly through the fear that the opposition of the Ulster members would split the Union. Despite brave resolutions on behalf of Irish independence in general, it paid no benefit to its Irish members, in particular, when they were dismissed for refusing to work trains carrying troops or munitions. This lack of working-class solidarity had provoked Arthur Griffith in the summer to complain: 'The English railway-men are conspiring with the English junkers.' He exaggerated, but he provided, in the event, a juster estimate of men like J. H. Thomas, the General Secretary of the National Union of Railwaymen, than those Conservatives who feared that Labour leaders of his kidney were about to launch the country into revolution. J. H. Thomas, who had come to Dublin seven months earlier in a futile attempt to persuade his members to carry troops and munitions, reappeared on the 15th December to organise the return to work.

Christmas was in the air, and all hopes of peace had not been lost. The party season was in full swing, while little gangs of desperate men waited on deserted roads, with an assortment of shotguns, revolvers and bombs, for a military or police patrol, and the police and military raided for documents and men on the run. Irish men and women went on with the dance, although occasionally a little group of I.R.A. gunmen invaded the genteel proceedings to stop the music and demand money or arms with menaces, or Black and Tans interrupted in search of 'Shinners' and free drink. One such raid on an I.R.A. dance in Limerick ended in a shooting affray in which five Volunteers and one Black and Tan were killed. Dubliners, meanwhile, enjoyed the play at the Abbey Theatre. Old gentlemen, who had prolonged their dinners at their clubs beyond the curfew hour, glanced apprehensively up and down the street, and made a run for home as though they were criminals. Diners looked up at the sound of an explosion, remarked 'that was a bomb', and returned, unmoved to their victuals. But even the most respectable and law-abiding could not be sure of avoiding trouble. A couple of Auxiliaries arrested a well-known Dublin business man while he was taking luncheon with the ex-High Sheriff and another Dublin worthy. 'You have bluffed us for a long time, Michael Collins,' one of the Auxiliaries said, 'but we have got you at last.' They dragged him, protesting, from his table and his friends and bore him off to Dublin Castle.

On Christmas Eve a party of Auxiliaries raided the

Gresham Hotel and nearly caught the real Michael Collins who was dining with one of his personal aides, Liam Tobin, Liam Mellowes, the I.R.A. Director of Purchases, Rory O'Connor, the Director of Engineering who had organised the arson attacks in Liverpool in November, and Gearoid O'Sullivan, the Adjutant-General. All were badly wanted men, but they were able to give a satisfactory account of themselves. Collins passed himself off as an accountant, with an office in Dame Street, and explained that a word, that looked like 'rifles' on the papers in his pocket, was really 'refills'. It may well have been so, for Michael Collins was a prodigious paper-worker. One Auxiliary was so suspicious that he produced a photograph of Collins from his own pocket and carefully compared the original with the reproduction; but Collins looked so like his description of himself, and so unlike the ruthless organiser of gunmen, that after a few nervous moments the Auxiliaries left. Collins and his companions celebrated this escape in one of his rare evenings of relaxation. Three of this happy band were to die violently, and on different sides, during the Civil War: Michael Collins in a Republican ambush or, as many believed, at the hand of an assassin of his own side, and Mellowes and O'Connor in front of an Irish Free State Army firing squad after five months in Mountjoy without trial.

The Irish were to prove that they had little to learn from either the Black and Tans or from Sir Henry Wilson, but at the end of 1920 the friends of Irish freedom could only see villainy on one side. De Valera, who arrived secretly in Dublin from the United States on this Christmas Eve, had expressed the generally accepted view shortly before his departure, in a speech at the Waldorf Astoria in New York:

If Britain wants to continue to overrun Ireland with Black and Tans, and to massacre the Irish people until even the British generals and statesmen themselves are compelled to cry out that their barbarities are worse than those of the Bashi-bazouks, surely Britain does not expect that the people of any self-respecting nation can covet her friendship.

The British Labour Party Commission expressed similar sentiments in its report which it delivered to a special conference in London on the 23rd December. It presented a picture of the Black and Tans and Auxiliaries 'compelling the whole Irish people—men, women and children—to live in an atmosphere of sheer terrorism' that caused amazement and delight among Sinn Fein propagandists. It found: 'Things that are being done in the name of Britain which must make her name stink in the nostrils of the whole world.' This was certainly true. It concluded: 'Only by granting to Ireland the freedom which is her due can our people fulfil their great responsibilities towards our sister nation'; but, to the astonishment of General Macready, it also recommended martial law as the most humane method of coercion. 'Until the report appeared,' Macready wrote, 'I had been under the impression that one of the main factors which deterred the Government from imposing martial law was the fear of the Labour Party in Great Britain.' General Sir Henry Lawson also made his report to the Peace with Ireland Council and found, after a tour on 'the Republican Scenic Railway', that: 'The spirit of the nation is behind the Sinn Fein organisation and no settlement can be really satisfactory which fails to secure the co-operation of the Sinn Fein movement.'

On the same day as the publication of the Labour Party report, the Government of Ireland Act establishing separate Parliaments for the Six Northern and Twenty-six Southern counties received the Royal Assent. Few people believed it would bring peace to Ireland; and no Irish peer had voted for it, but the representatives of Ulster accepted it as the better of two bad alternatives. It received little notice in the Press and the majority of Englishmen were more concerned, on that day, with the defeat of the M.C.C. in the first Test Match in Australia, and the imperative need of 'strengthening the tail' and of finding a new fast bowler. But behind the scenes in Dublin and London, peace feelers were still out. In Dublin, Father O'Flanagan was canvassing a scheme for an immediate settlement on the basis of Dominion Home Rule. Collins, who signed a very similar settlement a year later, strongly condemned Father O'Flanagan's efforts. In London, Lloyd George was still arguing the case for a one or two months' truce during which passions might cool and negotiation become possible. At a Cabinet meeting on the 29th December, at which the Cork burnings and the behaviour of the Black and Tans were discussed, Sir Henry Wilson pressed for martial law over the whole of Ireland. He found to his disgust that Winston Churchill, the Secretary for War, whom he had recorded as being 'in full blast for martial law' only five days earlier, had changed sides and now supported Lloyd George's proposals. Despite Sir Henry Wilson's arguments, the Cabinet refused even to grant a request from General Macready that the martial law area should be extended to Clare, Wexford, Waterford and Kilkenny. 'They *are* a miserable crowd. My contempt for their brains, knowledge, pluck and character deepens every day,' he wrote in his diary. 'They will ruin Ireland and the Empire. The suggestion tonight was that, by having a truce of two months, the rebels would be pacified and would not give any further trouble! Whew! I think we have scotched the plan of making a truce with rebels and murderers.'

There were men in Dublin and Cork, in Limerick and Tralee who would have said 'Amen' to that. They too, were not interested in a truce, but only in victory.

CHAPTER TEN

Die-Hards on the Defensive

THE IMPERIALIST VIEW from Westminster on the 1st January, 1921, did not suggest that it was going to be a happy year. The prospects were nearly everywhere unpleasing. At home there was a threat of a general strike; in the Middle East there was also the likelihood of Britain's involvement in a war between Turkey and Greece. In Cairo, Lord Milner proposed handing over the country to an Egyptian government; in Delhi, Edwin Montagu, the Secretary of State for India, showed distressing signs of sympathy for Indian nationalism; the Arabs in Mesopotamia were, meanwhile, still exhibiting a stubborn reluctance to come under the British wing. Above all, the Soviet Union showed no signs of the immediate collapse which had been prophesied by the experts.

To the predominantly die-hard majority at Westminster, all these threats to imperial security, at home and abroad, seemed to be different aspects of the universal enemy—Bolshevism. Sinn Fein was, of course, Bolshevik in this view. Both the Duke of Northumberland and Lord Carson had assured the House of Lords that Russian gold was behind the movement, and officials in Dublin Castle believed, but could not prove, that it was reaching Ireland through the Irish Labour Party, or through Sinn Fein agents in touch with Moscow. In this particular context the true-blue imperialist felt, with a certain logic, that to give way in Ireland would be to give way everywhere. The Irishmen, who had no other political aim than to secure control of their own parish pump, threatened to create a dangerous precedent, and in far-away India, Gandhi and Nehru were following their struggle with sympathy and interest. But Gandhi thought that the Irish were providing an object lesson on how not to deal with England. 'Even under the most adverse circumstances,' he said. 'I have found Englishmen amenable to reason and persuasion, and as they always wish to appear just it is easier to shame them than others into doing the right thing.' Sinn Fein's original programme of passive resistance might well have secured Ireland's independence and have spared the country much bloodshed and the horrors of a civil war, for the pro-Irish pressure of British public opinion was very strong and, in the end, decisive. At the beginning of 1921 the die-hards at Westminster would have liked to root out Sinn Fein with fire and steel, but the political, Press and public revulsion at the activities of the Black and Tans, and of the Auxiliaries, had already made it impossible for any government, which relied upon popular support, to adopt such a policy. The alternative was agreement by negotiation, sooner or later.

By New Year's Day, 1921, it was known that de Valera was back in Dublin, and parliamentary correspondents were officially inspired to report that his return would make negotiation easier. In a speech of welcome to a cross-country team from Cornell University, Sir Hamar Greenwood publicly anticipated an amicable settlement. In Dublin, General Macready was instructed by Sir John Anderson not to interfere with de Valera, nor to arrest him, and felt that 'it is quite impossible to carry out a repressive policy if we have one hand tied behind our back'. General Macready did not share Sir Hamar Greenwood's optimism.

De Valera had been away from Ireland for a year; he had to give his colleagues both an account of his adventures in the United States, and to learn from them of the changes in Irish affairs during his absence. His American tour had

not achieved its main object, which was to persuade either
the Democrats or the Republicans, or both, to adopt the
cause of Irish independence as part of their political programme in the Presidential elections. He raised the impressive sum of three million dollars for the Dáil Loan, but
he also did signal service to the British Government by
dividing Irish Americans into two vociferously hostile
camps. His opponents there labelled him as 'the half-breed
Spaniard' and 'somebody's child from Spain' in a bout of
name-calling which was not always so polite. But his hopes
for the cause were not limited to appeals to Americans, and,
undeterred by the prevailing anti-Bolshevik hysteria, he
had conducted negotiations with the Soviet Russian
delegation which was also seeking recognition at Washington. After some discussion, preliminary heads of agreement
for an Irish-Soviet treaty had been drafted; a copy of this
document was later discovered in a raid in Dublin and
published in a White Paper, to confirm the darkest suspicions
at Westminster. But no Russian gold flowed into the Irish
Republican coffers. The traffic was the other way, and the
sum of 20,000 dollars was secretly loaned from the Treasury
of the Irish Republican Mission to the Soviet Mission in the
United States, who gave some pieces of smuggled jewellery
as security. The Irish Government still possesses part of the
Russian Crown Jewels as a memorial to the negotiations for
what might have been a most interesting political alliance.

De Valera seemed, to the die-hards of the Irish Republican Army, to be out of touch with the temper of the times.
He issued an address to the Irish people: 'Let us face the
New Year of the Republic ready to endure whatever yet
may be necessary to win for those who come after us the
priceless boon of permanent peace, and secure liberty in
their native land.' But his appreciation of the I.R.A.'s
campaign, and its effects, was distressing, particularly to
Cathal Brugha, the Defence Minister, who believed that
the I.R.A. could, unaided, drive the British into the sea. At

a meeting of the Dáil in the third week of January, de Valera said that the enemy had got superior forces, and all that Ireland had was the power of moral resistance. The question was: how far could they keep the people up to this resistance? He thought that their policy should be to stick on, to show no change on the outside as far as possible, and at the same time to make the burden on the people as light as they could. He felt that this policy might mean a lightening of their attacks on the enemy. This proposal was bitterly opposed by all but two of the members of the Dáil, Roger Sweetman, who had supported the truce negotiations, and Liam de Roiste (William Roche) of Cork. Collins said that 'it was not the parts of the country that fought hardest that were getting the worst hammering, but those that lay down under it'—a statement he repeated so often that, presumably, he believed it, although much of his time and energy were devoted to often futile attempts to stir up trouble in quiescent areas. The war parties were once more in command, both in Dublin and in London.

The peacemakers had still not given up all hope of an early settlement. Father O Flanagan went to London to discuss with Lloyd George his proposals for an immediate settlement on the lines of Dominion status, against the advice both of Collins and de Valera. This latest move towards peace had been engineered by 'Andy' Cope, as he was generally known, the Assistant Under-Secretary for Ireland, who was Lloyd George's unofficial agent, and later to be rewarded with a knighthood and the secretary-ship of the Liberal Party. He pursued his contacts in the Sinn Fein organisation with all the skill and persistence he had acquired as a Customs detective, and with such energy and fearlessness that he was accused of favouring the Sinn Fein cause, and even, by an angry peer in the House of Lords, of betraying military secrets to the I.R.A. This energetic civil servant, who had the gift of unintentionally reducing staff officers to speechless rage by the use of a

few ill-chosen words, was the man who was largely responsible for the truce that was negotiated six months later
on much the same terms. But in January, 1921, Collins
could only regret that Father O Flanagan was allowing
himself 'to be made a tool of a pleasant gentleman like
Cope'.

His apprehensions were unnecessary. The Coalition
Cabinet, which vacillated constantly between coercion and
negotiation, on the 4th January changed its decision of five
days earlier, and granted General Macready's request for the
extension of martial law to Clare, Wexford, Waterford and
Kilkenny. In Cork, on New Year's Day, General Strickland
had ordered the first official reprisals, and seven houses in
Middelton had been blown up after an I.R.A. attack,
because, it was officially explained, the inhabitants were
bound to have known of the ambush and attack, and that
they had neglected to give any information, either to the
military or to the police authorities. If they had given
information, their bodies would have been found by the
roadside labelled 'spies and traitors beware'. The unhappy
non-belligerent population often had, in this way, to choose
between death and the destruction of their property.

This first official reprisal caused indignation in England.
The Daily News commented: 'It is a savage outrage upon
human decency', and quoted from a speech which Lloyd
George had made in December, 1900, during the Boer War,
in which he had said: 'In regard to military reprisals,
nothing is gained by making a man desperate. It is a silly,
foolish, iniquitous policy to burn his farm, ruin his property,
and bring his family to the grave. It is not a military question at all. It is a question of understanding the ordinary
influences that govern human nature.' *The Westminster
Gazette* made another point in a leader: 'This new system
denies to suspected accomplices the elementary rights which
are extended even to the principal criminals themselves.'
The Labour Party organised mass demonstrations in

Manchester, Glasgow and Cardiff to condemn reprisals and call for an Irish Constituent Assembly. The execution of the first Volunteer to be sentenced to death under martial law caused further misgivings, and it seemed to so eminent a legal authority as Sir John Simon 'to be a very serious question whether the military authority in Ireland can define new grounds for capital punishment'. Another six Volunteers were shot in Cork at the end of February, and their deaths provoked the Bishop of Cork, who had excommunicated the murderers of policemen, to declare: 'The Government think they will break the spirit of the young men of Ireland by these executions. They will only succeed in driving everyone into the ranks of the I.R.A. as they drove the country into the arms of Sinn Fein in 1916. It is shocking to execute these young men when their organisation and action were provoked by mis-government.'

Martial law did not, as Dr. Cohalan feared, drive everyone into the I.R.A., but so great was the strain imposed by the constant attacks, the reprisals and the counter-reprisals, that the intake of patients with mental breakdown greatly increased at the Cork Asylum during the first weeks of 1921. The organisation and action of the I.R.A., to which the Bishop referred, varied in effectiveness. 'Your average ambusher,' a British Intelligence officer told a correspondent, 'is an ignorant peasant who has a gun put into his hand, is herded off to the scene of the ambush, and told to loose it off. That sort bolts at the first opportunity.' But there were more effective opponents. The Flying Columns and the Active Service Units of the I.R.A. had been training hard throughout the autumn and winter months of 1920; they were generally well disciplined, and had developed, in many areas, into efficient guerilla units.

Martial law did not swell their numbers, but it stiffened their resolve. If the penalty for being armed was death, there was no point in surrender. They were desperately short of arms, and were equipped with an assortment of weapons, including Hotchkiss machine guns, captured Lewis guns, German Mausers, Mannlichers, Winchester repeaters, British Army Lee-Enfields, and a variety of sporting guns including rook rifles and blunderbusses which had long since ceased to figure in gunsmiths' catalogues. It needed courage to undertake any action against well-equipped troops and police with this varied, and usually inadequate, armament. Their ammunition included German, French, Swiss and British cartridges, and the soft-nosed and split-nosed bullets which inflicted terrible wounds, and had been condemned by The Hague Convention on the Laws and Customs of War. The majority of the Volunteers, who prided themselves on their soldierly correctness, had probably never heard of The Hague, and still less of the Convention, but the use of this internationally outlawed ammunition provoked violent antagonism among the Crown Forces. 'The swine!' an officer remarked to a correspondent. 'If I caught one of them with these things on him I'd shoot him in cold blood with the greatest of pleasure.'

Streams of despatches and orders flowed from the Brigades in the field to Michael Collins in his office in Mespil Road, Dublin, and from the Brigades to subordinate units. A close watch was kept on movements, not only of troops, but of individuals who had attracted the notice of the I.R.A. One sergeant, of the auxiliaries, for example, collected a dossier which travelled ahead of him to the Volunteer headquarters whenever he left one station for another. 'Ex-Lieutenant British Army. 3 wound stripes,' part of the record reads. 'Heavy boozer, went to Thurles for a few months—a bit busy using day patrols and generally assaulted people there. He was involved in shootings in Upperchurch before he went back to Dublin. He has returned to the South, and has been in two more shootings in Limerick and Thurles.' 'Everybody wanted to get him,' a Dublin business man, who was once a Volunteer, recalls, 'but we never did.'

Information of every kind went through the I.R.A. Intelligence sieve: everybody knows what everyone is doing in country districts. Two members of the Dublin Castle 'murder gang' arrive in Templemore and are immediately noticed. Girls are walking out with peelers in another district and are reported: their names and addresses, and, if possible, their photographs must be secured and appropriate action taken. Some tenants are still paying their rents to English landlords; they must be stopped. There are reports that a party of Auxiliaries goes to fetch the milk for their barracks at six o clock every evening with a look-out in one village; that in another, 'Captain Haddock, 1/o Ordinance Barracks, walks out Military Road to Miss Conray, evidently to court'. Here were two more opportunities for striking a blow for the freedom of Ireland.

'Practically all over the country opportunities for minor activities occur,' *An t-Oglach*, the official organ of the Volunteers, explained in an article entitled 'The Value of "Small Jobs".' It cited three examples in Dublin: a sniper with a Mauser smashed a searchlight—'a complex lens and silvered reflecting mirror worth together twelve hundred pounds': a cyclist scout on the Rathmines Road 'jumped off his machine, drew an automatic, while pretending to adjust the gear of his bicycle, and shot dead the Auxiliary sentry outside Lissonfield House, wounding another': three Volunteers attacked two enemy despatch bearers, shot one of them, and captured a fine motor bicycle, and a Webley revolver with five rounds in it.' The article concluded with the injunction: 'Take care of the pence and the pounds will take care of themselves.' It was not the frequency of these attacks, but the possibility of their occurrence at any time that so demoralised the Crown Forces.

Conditions in Ireland were favourable to guerilla activity

38. The burning of Cork, 11th December, 1920: Early next morning citizen's review the results in Patrick Street. They do not know that Sir Hamar Greenwood will accuse them of setting fire to their own city. An Auxiliary testified five days later: 'I am at present in bed recovering from a severe chill contracted on Saturday night last during the burning and looting of Cork in all of which I took perforce a reluctant part. We did it all right.' General Macready was of the same opinion.

39. The wreck of a shopping centre: A witness reports on the destruction of a jeweller's shop: 'The loot of Hilser's continued throughout the night at different periods by police or Black and Tans. About 1.30 a.m. a party of them broke every bit of glass in Hilser's and with the aid of flash-lamps which they used inside I could see them looting the entire shop. The party consisted of men in civilian attire, Black and Tans or R.I.C. and two soldiers. They had large kitbags which they filled with the loot.'

First, the military had, as General Macready complained, 'one hand tied behind our back'. The Army was not allowed to engage in the kind of campaign that is politely called 'pacification'. Of the relatively small number of men sentenced to death under martial law, only fourteen were executed between the 1st February, 1921, and the Truce on the 11th July. In all, the British Government executed twenty-four Republicans between November, 1920, and June, 1921, compared with the seventy-seven shot by order of the Irish Free State during the Civil War between November, 1921, and May, 1922. Secondly, the Volunteers could count on the support of the general population. In a nationalist, as opposed to a political, insurrection, even people of opposing views do not commonly betray their own countrymen and, in Ireland, the bodies labelled 'spies and informers beware' were a powerful additional argument in favour of co-operation. Thirdly, the country, with its poor communications and stretches of bog and mountain land, was ideal for guerilla action, and the Volunteers could nearly always, if hard pressed, hide their arms and merge with the civilian population.

At the beginning of 1921, the laying of ambushes was no longer the comparatively safe operation that it had been in the summer and autumn of 1920. A training school for guerilla tactics had been established at the Curragh for British officers and N.C.O.'s, and both the police and troops began to move out into the country after the Flying Columns. An extract from a report by a young member of a Flying Column admirably catches the temper and spirit of these changed times:

Enemy activity was now very intense, and the noise of buzzing lorries dropping fresh troops all around in our vicinity pointed to the fact that we were surely discovered. Observation scouts were posted on a haybarn in the adjoining field and a few on trees and scoured the locality with field-glasses. These tactics were adopted for a distance of miles. Entering the little field in which we were positioned was a small gate, and suddenly we noticed through the foliage of our hiding place an old Colonel wearing a fur coat and cap, and another Officer advancing into the field. The Colonel levelled his field-glasses on every part of the field and now Séan whispered every man to be perfectly motionless. Now the Colonel entered into conversation with the other Officer and after ten minutes or so they both withdrew.

Military activities still continued until suddenly we heard three rapid successive rifle shots and saw Very lights go up from the direction of the school-house. They were answered from different directions. Séan was of the opinion that this was a possible signal for attack and that we had been discovered. He addressed us with stirring words which fired us in our hour of peril. He placed the facts and our position before us in their truest form, and explained his hopes and fears. Nothing remained but for us to die bravely like valiant soldiers of The Republic. He told us to fire accurately and collectively and let each bullet be a missile of death. He explained that in any case death was inevitable and consequently he wished to make the enemy purchase a dearly bought victory. He ordered that no man should break away unless instructions to that effect were given, as no possible chance of escape through the enemy's ranks was feasible since we were encircled in a perfect network of military cordons. From early morning until evening all males from fifteen to seventy years were arrested and taken to local centres for identification purposes, consequently all hope of escape was vague. The signals continued from different directions for almost an hour and yet no sign of attack.

The suspense and anxiety were even more nerve-racking than an actual engagement. Seeing that no attack was forthcoming, Séan realised that we had not yet been discovered, and that the signals were in all possibility for withdrawal of troops. This proved correct and renewed activity in the ranks of the foot troops stationed in front, directly in our view, was noticed by us and our hopes of safety were again in jeopardy, till finally we noticed that they began to withdraw. Our hopes again soared and our leader strengthened them by assuring us that the signals were signals of the enemy's retreat. Every man felt proud that day more than ever of our gallant leader Séan, young in years, so cool and brave and yet old in experience. All would have willingly died for him and with him. For more than an hour the retreat continued, and finally when all had withdrawn we could scarcely credit that we had escaped. The age of miracles was by no means dead as that round-up proved in our case. Friendly Cumann na m'Ban brought us refreshments, tea, etc., in buckets and needless to say hunger proved a good sauce, and it was gladly received. We had been fasting from 9.30 the night before, as in our hurried retreat that morning we had not partaken of breakfast. We had maintained our cramped, motionless positions all day to 5.30 p.m., and many were lying on damp surfaces which had penetrated through clothing, causing stiffness and aching limbs.

A Flying Column of the 1st Cork Brigade was less fortunate when it was surrounded and attacked in a farm house on the 20th February by a mixed force of Auxiliaries and soldiers. Five Volunteers were killed in the action before they surrendered, and the Auxiliaries shot seven of their prisoners and were about to kill the rest when the commanding officer of the troops intervened to save them.

The Volunteers learned their soldiering in the tough, but effective, school of actual experience. Very few of them were ex-servicemen. Their spirit and discipline were excellent when they were led by such resourceful and determined commanders as Liam Lynch, Séan McKeon, Tom Barry and Ernie O'Malley. Unlike the Auxiliaries, they usually treated their prisoners well and even released them, except when they shot them as hostages; and they did what they could for the wounded. They were inspired by a fierce idealism that could persuade them that the most squalid murder was an act of the highest heroism. 'We were now hard, cold and ruthless as our enemy had been since hostilities began,' Tom Barry has recorded. 'The British were met with their own weapons. They had gone down into the mire to destroy us and our nation, and down after them we had to go to stop them. The step was not an easy one, for one's mind was darkened and one's outlook made bleak by the decisions which had to be taken.'

It is, unhappily, not always possible to go into the mire without sinking deeper, and the execution of real and supposed spies and informers became exercises in sadism. Seventy-three were shot between the 1st January and the end of April. One of these victims was Mrs. Lindsay, of Coachford, in County Cork, an old lady over seventy years of age. The circumstances of her death provided a sad commentary on the state of Ireland, and provoked a momentary revulsion against Sinn Fein. An informer told her that an ambush was being prepared by the local I.R.A. She told the police, and her informer then informed against her to the I.R.A. Volunteers of the 1st Cork Brigade arrested her, and threatened to shoot her as a reprisal unless six men condemned to death were reprieved. General Macready felt that he could not strike this bargain, which, as he explained, 'would have resulted in the kidnapping of loyal or influential persons every time a death sentence was passed on a rebel.' Michael Collins was distressed at the adverse publicity caused by her death, and explained later that he would not have allowed the execution if he had known she was so old, but did not define the permissible age limits within which women could be shot as hostages.

The shooting by Dublin Volunteers of some British Army mules and horses caused even greater dismay among animal lovers in England, although Sinn Fein propagandists gave an assurance that the death of the victims had been instantaneous.

Meanwhile, the succession of attacks and reprisals continued on a restricted, but more concentrated, scale than in the campaigns of 1920. A District Inspector of the Royal Irish Constabulary and his wife were shot in Mallow; as a reprisal a party of Auxiliaries shot up the railway station, killing three railwaymen and wounding five others. To work, or to travel, on the railways was becoming hazardous and ambushes were frequent, although erratic in their action. In one attack in February, two Auxiliaries were killed, and in another six civilians. Volunteers were also blocking roads, blowing up bridges and cutting down telegraph poles on a large scale in the South and West. Limerick Volunteers ambushed a lorry load of Black and Tans, killing eleven and wounding two. The Black and Tans retaliated by burning farms and houses, and in West Cork the Volunteers burned two Loyalist houses for every Sinn Fein house destroyed. Loyalists who were unable to sell their houses stayed on in fear of death, either at the hands of the I.R.A. or of the freelances amongst the peasantry who coveted their cattle and lands. Their premonitions were often justified, and few people could be sure of avoiding trouble from one side or the other. Even so distinguished a Loyalist as Lord Dunsany, the Irish landlord and man of letters, was fined £25 at a British court martial for having arms and ammunition 'not under proper control', in spite of a spirited defence in which he declared: 'I have fought against Sinn Fein, the Boers and the Germans.' Six soldiers were shot in Cork while walking out with girls, and a Black and Tan patrol, firing wildly from a Crossley tender, killed a fourteen-year-old boy and wounded an eleven-year-old and a nine-year-old, who were playing hurley in a field. Attacks were made on police and soldiers in Dublin, where large parts of the city were periodically cordoned off with barbed wire, tanks and armoured cars, while Auxiliaries, Black and Tans and soldiers combed the streets and brought out all young men for closer scrutiny.

These were some of the events of the first few weeks of 1921 in a country which, at that time, was as much a part of the United Kingdom as Wales or Scotland. In the English newspapers they overshadowed even such a dramatic report as that the Americans were about to launch a rocket to the moon on the 15th February, or such a down-to-earth announcement, a few days later, that the unemployed figure stood at a million and a half, and that unemployed benefit was going to be cut to fifteen shillings a week for men and to twelve shillings for women. *The Manchester Guardian* reprinted a report by Judge Bodkin, of Clare, who detailed one hundred and thirty-nine cases of criminal injury by Crown Forces for which he had awarded compensation of £187,046. The Associated Locomotive Engineers and Firemen threatened to strike if their demand for an enquiry into the shooting of railwaymen at Mallow was not granted; but there was no enquiry and no strike. The Labour Party issued twelve million leaflets demanding the withdrawal of troops from Ireland, and Mr. Arthur Greenwood, one of its leaders, said at a mass rally in the Albert Hall: 'We see a country torn to pieces by the deliberate policy of the Government with a trail of burnings and scenes of devastation which remind us of the war areas.' Anxiety about the Government's policy was by no means confined to the United Kingdom, and on the 19th February General Smuts declared: 'Unless the Irish question is settled on the great principles which form the basis of this Empire, this Empire must cease to exist.'

I.R.A. Volunteers in England also hoped to bring the

plight of their country to the notice of English people by reprisals. During two week-ends in February, Volunteers raided villages and burned farmhouses in the Manchester area, and on the 18th February three Irish youths were convicted at the Old Bailey of attempted arson at the Vacuum Oil Works in Wandsworth, and of firing at the police. 'We intended,' one of them said, 'trying means which might draw attention to arson in Ireland.' In spite of these acts, which created no sympathy for the Irish cause, the pressure of public opinion made itself felt at Westminster. On the 21st February, Captain Wedgwood Benn moved an amendment in the debate on the address: 'That the policy and practice pursued by the Executive in Ireland have failed to secure the repression of organised outrage, have involved the officers and servants of the Crown in a competition in crime with the offenders against the law, have handed over to the military authorities an unrestricted discretion in the definition and punishment of offence, and have frustrated the prospects of an agreed settlement of the problem of Irish Self-Government.' The Government was in no danger of defeat, but the division of Ayes 87 and Noes 257 was a serious reverse for Lloyd George. Two-thirds of the Coalition Liberals abstained from voting, and seven voted against the Government. Of the forty-three who voted for the Government, twenty-one either held office or were secretaries to Ministers.

Debates on Ireland in the House of Commons had fallen into a stereotyped pattern, with the recital of atrocities committed by the Crown Forces, particularly by Black and Tans and the Auxiliaries, on one side, and denunciation of the 'murder gang' on the other. This debate was no exception. Truth was often a casualty in these exchanges. Any stick was good enough for beating the opponents, and no attempt was made to verify the charges and counter-charges supplied by Sinn Fein propagandists and the authorities at Dublin Castle. Michael Collins used to boast that he could always get a question asked in the House of Commons, and Commander Kenworthy, later Lord Strabolgi, was his chief, self-appointed, spokesman. Kenworthy was a man of generous spirit, but he was prepared to believe any story, however preposterous, as long as it was against the Government. He contented himself on this occasion with barracking Government speakers and provoking cries of 'Order' and 'Shut up'. But the bare facts, without distortion or exaggeration, were on the side of the Opposition, and Mr. Asquith, the leader of the Opposition Liberals, made good use of them in a speech in which he said:

'The real vindication, or attempted vindication of the policy so unhappily pursued during the last six months is that it has succeeded, or has good prospects of success. The Prime Minister gave us an almost glowing, at any rate, an exuberant description, of the advance which has been made in the direction of pacification and the suppression of crime. What are the facts? At the very moment that the Prime Minister was speaking an hon. friend sitting beside me put into my hands a telegram which had come from Ireland that day describing how within a few miles of the City of Cork two trains were ambushed and a number of soldiers and civilians lost their lives. If you look in the newspaper today you will see that within the last ten days in the City of Cork, not in the hills, not in the outlying regions, five citizens were shot dead. Only yesterday there was an open fight in the town of Middleton, in which thirteen people—I believe the number has since been added to—were killed. This is a deplorable commentary on the allegation that the policy of reprisals has been a success. Only this afternoon the Chief Secretary himself told us that civilian judges could not safely be entrusted with the duty of adjudicating in criminal cases, and that witnesses dare not come forward and give evidence for fear of their lives.'

Conditions in Ireland were disturbing enough to make a few Conservatives cross the floor of the House. Of these, the most notable was Lord Robert Cecil who, in a thoughtful speech in the same debate, warned the House that the Government's policy was turning moderates into extremists, and that Cardinal Logue, who, with the assistance of his priests had been doing his best to keep Ireland quiet, could not hope to make the attempt much longer. Sir Hamar Greenwood was called 'the chief trombone of the ministerial orchestra' by one member, and was derided by others for his constantly repeated assurances that the condition of Ireland was improving. He had so compromised himself that he was not even half-believed when he was almost telling the truth. A statement of his that 'there is as great peace as there is in the county of Kent in three-quarters of Ireland' caused particular delight to Opposition members. It was an exaggeration but it was much nearer the truth than the picture of a country ravaged like war-torn Belgium. But despite his oratorical gifts, Sir Hamar was unable, on this occasion, to excite enthusiasm among his supporters even when he quoted, with the full power of his emotive utterance, the words of an appeal which the Bishop of Kilmore had recently made in Ireland in a pastoral letter:

'O young men of the diocese, what has come over some of you? You were religious, you were virtuous, you hearkened to the teaching of the Church. You were noble hearted, pure minded, chivalrous and generous. What Devil's doctrine has gripped your minds, darkened your conscience, steeled your heart, that at the bidding of anyone you should pour out the blood of one of God's human beings?'

The Daily News the next day reported bluntly that 'the House is tired of Sir Hamar Greenwood's bluff, bounce and bluster' and printed a specially commissioned poem by Sir William Watson, a poet who was knighted for his services to literature in 1917, but whose work is now so little read that his centenary in 1958 went unnoticed. It was entitled *England's Choice*, the first verse reading:

> Yonder where shakes with antic laughter
> In elfin moonlight the spoilful sea,
> What shall the stars behold hereafter
> Ireland captive or Ireland free?

In more prosaic terms, many people inside and outside the House of Commons asked: 'How much longer is it going on?'

The same question agitated the minds of many of the speakers in the House of Lords' debate on the address on the 22nd February. Lord Buckmaster, in an able speech, summarised the standpoint of the Opposition and demanded the withdrawal, or reconstruction, of the Black and Tans. Lord Birkenhead, speaking for the Government at some length, expressed the Government's policy pithily, in one sentence: 'Without a vigorous assertion of force, you cannot cure the mischiefs in Ireland today.' He also recommended to the attention of Sinn Fein 'the sublime admonitions of the Sermon on the Mount'.

Dr. Davidson, the Archbishop of Canterbury, took up a central position that did not wholly please either side. This distinguished and respected prelate had intervened more than once during the Great War to prevent reprisals which had, in his words, 'as a deliberate object the killing and wounding of noncombatants. In his speech, he praised the Royal Irish Constabulary and was sure that it was true to its splendid tradition and had done, and was doing, heroic service. 'No epithets are too forcible,' he said, 'or too unsparing for us to use in characterising the cowardice, cruelty, sometimes the barbaric cruelty, and the insane wickedness which these men have to oppose and put down. On these gangs must rest the fearful responsibility for the present mischief in Ireland.' These were honeyed words for the Government supporters, but, turning to the subject of the Black and Tans, he added, in a plea for common sense: 'To speak of some action in Ireland today as intolerable because it would be intolerable in Piccadilly Circus would be the merest pedantry. We go back to the elementary principle of right and wrong, of ethics, not politics. I must reiterate what we must have said here before that you cannot justifiably punish wrong-doing by lawlessly doing the like. Not by calling in the devil, will you cast out devils or punish devilry.'

Many priests in Ireland had been making the same point. On the 13th February, members of the Irish Hierarchy condemned the repression by the Crown Forces in Pastorals read that day, and at the same time urged the people to refrain from acts of violence. A fortnight earlier Dr. Gilmartin, the Bishop of Galway, who had urged his flock to surrender their arms, had said of an ambush at Headford in which three Black and Tans were killed and three wounded: 'The misguided criminals who fired a few shots from behind a wall and then decamped to a safe distance are guilty of a triple crime. They have broken the truce of God, they have incurred the guilt of murder.' Dr. Cohalan, the Bishop of Cork, who called a spade a spade to the distress of both sides, and particularly to the I.R.A., went still further and wrote: 'Was the proclamation of an Irish Republic by the Sinn Fein members of Parliament... sufficient to constitute Ireland a Republic, according to our Church teaching? I answer: It was not.'

Dr. Alfred O'Rahilly, who, according to Tom Barry, 'was one of the most learned men in Europe, and probably the greatest lay exponent of Catholic Action and Sociology in Ireland', had been refuting the Bishop point by point on behalf of the I.R.A. ever since his excommunication of the murderers of policemen, and had 'completely clarified the position for those in doubt'. The relations between Sinn Fein and the Catholic bishops had been engaging de Valera's attention since his return from America, and he tried throughout the spring and summer of 1921 to secure the Church's recognition of the Republic, but without success. On the 2nd February he had written to the Archbishop of New York, who was in Rome at the time, urging him to use his influence to prevent a Papal rescript against Sinn Fein; later in the month he drafted an appeal to the Hierarchy, setting out the claims for the Republic, and asking the bishops to wait for an explanation from the Dáil before denouncing crimes.

Meanwhile, two events which had occurred on the 9th February had lit the fuse which was to set off another explosion in the House of Commons at the end of the month, although these were neither more nor less discreditable than many other outrages. On that night a party of Auxiliaries raided the shop of a Mr. and Mrs. Chandler, a Unionist couple, near Trim in County Meath; they were searching for hidden ammunition. They helped themselves liberally to the drinks in the shop, then stripped the counters of a side of bacon, ten chickens, two bags of candles, a quantity of condensed milk, two hundredweight of sugar, bottles of milk, whisky, rum, port, ale, champagne and twenty-three bottles of brandy; they also robbed the till of five sovereigns. From upstairs they took a white counterpane, a quilt and some blankets, four pairs of sheets, two field glasses, two gold watches, two gold bracelets, ten silver forks, a silver watch and a gold brooch. They damaged the pony trap and put four bullets into the water butt before piling into their lorries with the loot. At the time Mrs. Chandler estimated the loss and damage at £325, but this undisciplined raid on a spirit grocers soon became known, by a rapid process of exaggeration, as 'the notorious looting of Trim', and was spoken of in the same terms as the burning of Cork.

On the same night two young Irishmen were arrested in Dublin and taken to the Castle. At midnight an Auxiliary

Commander, by the name of King, drove with two cadets out of Dublin, taking the two prisoners. The prisoners were found next morning, one dead and the other dying, in a field near Drumcondra, on the outskirts of the city. General Crozier went first to Trim where he summarily tried twenty-six Auxiliary cadets, held back five for trial and dismissed twenty-one. He returned to Dublin to find that an enquiry was to be held into the Drumcondra shootings, but that, or so he claimed later, the evidence had been rigged.

Meanwhile, the dismissed Auxiliaries plotted their return to Ireland from London. They used the Long Bar at the Trocadero as their headquarters, where they were advised by their ringleader, who later achieved a certain notoriety as a Soviet agent, to threaten 'to blow the gaff' about conditions in Ireland, and, in particular the burning of Cork, if they were not reinstated. In Dublin, General Tudor, who was in command of the Police Forces, was not satisfied with General Crozier's conduct of the trial. He had, already in November, deprived Crozier of the power to dismiss Auxiliaries, and had for some time been considering relieving him of his appointment. The twenty-six cadets were reinstated, and on the 25th February General Crozier resigned, to make the front-page story in most of the London Press, and to occupy several columns with the account of his unjust treatment by General Tudor and of the irregularities committed by the men under his own command. In February, 1921, the word of this bull-necked, loquacious, and over-excitable soldier was taken for gospel; but when, a few years later, Desmond McCarthy incorporated some of Crozier's charges against General Tudor in *Lord Oxford's Letters to a Friend*, he was threatened with an action for libel. McCarthy found, on investigation, that the charges had no foundation, and not only issued a public apology and deleted the offending passages from the book, but also wrote to General Tudor: 'I constantly think of my escape with amazed relief and gratitude. Think of it! If you had taken action, I should have been fighting shoulder to shoulder with Crozier. It would have been painfully true of my position then: "His honour rooted in dishonour stood".'

General Crozier went to see Commander Kenworthy, M.P., who told a meeting of Bermondsey Liberals after the interview: 'If the people knew the truth of what was going on in Ireland, they would throw the present Government out in a week.' *The Times*, *The Manchester Guardian*, *The Observer* and other papers demanded the resignation of Sir Hamar Greenwood, and also a public enquiry into General Crozier's resignation. But the Opposition soon became disillusioned with their new champion. 'They tell me that you are as much a murderer as any of them,' Mrs. Asquith said to General Crozier as they strolled the lawn before lunch at Sutton Courtenay, 'only you like things done in an orderly manner, and at Trim they were disorderly.' But yet, whether he was a reliable witness or not, Crozier's resignation served to draw attention once more to the activities of the Black and Tans and the Auxiliaries. *The Times* commented: 'We have long known that the Auxiliary Division was designed for a purpose which we have regarded as foolish and immoral, and that the very nature of its employment renders discipline in its ranks almost impossible.'

The 'Trim scandal' was debated in the House of Commons, where the usual repetitive exchanges were enlivened by the news that two of the Auxiliaries held back for trial had broken out and robbed a publican. The House was not reassured when Sir Hamar Greenwood explained that they had not been confined as prison accommodation was exhausted 'owing to the number of cadets under close arrest'. Five of the Auxiliaries were eventually convicted, and nineteen were returned to duty. Three Auxiliaries were tried in April for the Drumcondra murders, but, as in other such cases in Ireland and elsewhere, there was no evidence to convict.

The Trim looting, the Drumcondra murders and the dismissal of General Crozier put the Government on the defensive. The Opposition was beginning to prevail and uneasiness to manifest itself in the divided Cabinet; the Lord President of the Council, A. J. Balfour, an ex-Secretary for Ireland, an ex-Conservative Prime Minister and a member of the influential Cecil family, questioned the system of using Black and Tans and Auxiliaries. As Foreign Secretary in 1917, he had created a problem that was to be even more troublesome than Ireland when he promised the Jews a national home in Palestine. Even the autocratic Lord Curzon, the Foreign Secretary and ex-Viceroy of India, one of the most powerful Conservative figures, expressed his disgust at the conduct of affairs in Ireland; three months earlier he had justified reprisals in the House of Lords when he spoke of there being: 'in Ireland a criminal and ferocious conspiracy, the agents of which show no scruple or remorse, and who operate by methods which would disgrace a Hottentot in the bush. Soldiers and police are engaged in an heroic struggle face to face with death. We see them sometimes hitting back.' The Conservative Member for Ripon, who was later to hold the same high offices as Lord Curzon, made a speech in the House early in March which illustrated the anxiety felt by many Government supporters. He was Mr. Edward Wood, later to be better known as Lord Irwin, Viceroy of India, and as Lord Halifax, Foreign Secretary and British Ambassador to the United States. He said: 'When the first charges of reprisals were made, I refused to believe them, and it was in that attitude of mind that I voted for the Restoration of Order in Ireland Bill; but I do not hesitate to say that the cumulative effect of what has happened has made that intellectual attitude impossible to maintain. (Labour cheers). It is quite idle to deny that, making whatever allowances we like, there have been happenings by a section of the Crown's officers of which every Englishman must be ashamed.'

There were cynics, or realists, in Ireland who did not particularly value the generous sentiments expressed in the House of Commons. They judged people by their actions and not by their words and observed that some of the members, who were so hot about abuses in Ireland, had not been so scrupulous when they were in office. Mr. Asquith, their present self-appointed champion, for example, had been the Prime Minister responsible for the executions in 1916 and for the deportation, without trial, of 1,836 people. Mr. Henderson, the Labour leader, who now spoke so frequently in their cause, had been a member of that government, and had not been heard to protest at the time; and Lloyd George, whom Asquith castigated as the villain of the piece, was the Prime Minister, who, in 1917, released the prisoners whom Asquith had deported. It is understandable that there were some Irishmen who thought there was not much to choose between one Englishman and another, even if he were a Welshman, and that they would like to see the back of the lot.

CHAPTER ELEVEN

Mailed Fist and Olive Branch

IFTY-NINE POLICE and nine soldiers had been killed in the first two months of 1921. These casualty figures, which were, within a body or two, the same as those for the three summer months of July to September 1920, showed that there was plenty of fight left in the Irish Republican Army, although they suggested that the state of Ireland was very much worse than in fact it was. A bold young party of cyclists of the Clarion Club, a Labour Youth organisation, decided to go to Ireland to see for themselves, after attending a mass rally of protest at the Albert Hall against the Government's policy in Ireland. During the first week of March they toured the war areas in the South and West. They were told of many dreadful things that had happened, they saw a number of burned buildings and had to lift their bicycles over trenches cut in the roads by the I.R.A. They never heard a shot fired but were, at least, held up by an Auxiliary who, when forthrightly accused by these young cyclists of vilely oppressing the Irish people, asked plaintively: 'What could I do? I was wounded three times in Flanders, and all I could get to do when I came home was this dirty job.' They had plenty to report when they returned to England, but what they had heard from Labour platforms did not altogether accord with what they had seen.

Another visitor, who discounted much of what he read in the papers, was, on the other hand, surprised, as he emerged from a shop, to see three Auxiliaries shot down a hundred yards from Dublin Castle. A newspaper placard of a local paper in Cork perhaps helps to catch the curious atmosphere of this period. It read:

THE WEEK'S WARFARE

———

MURDER BY INSANE PROFESSOR

———

CAUGHT AT DRILL

———

FIVE CIVILIANS KILLED

———

GARDENING AND POULTRY NOTES

———

TALKS ON HEALTH

———

ALL THE USUAL FEATURES

———

By the beginning of March the Black and Tan reinforcements to the Royal Irish Constabulary numbered nearly seven thousand, bringing the full establishment up to fifteen thousand, the highest figure for many years. The deficiencies in their uniform had been made up, but they were still known as the Black and Tans and were proud of the name, although soldiers often called them the 'Black and Scums'. The Auxiliaries had also reached their full strength of fifteen hundred.

A serious attempt had been made to instil discipline into these forces, and since the beginning of the year over two hundred Black and Tans and over fifty Auxiliaries had been dismissed the service. A dozen also received sentences of from three to ten years' penal servitude, and nearly a hundred of them sentences from one month to two years. General Macready's threat of inflicting the death penalty on the Crown Forces was only executed once when an Auxiliary was hanged for murder. But discipline cannot be enforced merely by penalties, and there was a serious lack of good officers. The War Office tried to remedy this deficiency by offering Reserve Officers commands in the R.I.C., but there were few takers. In spite of their bad name, the great majority of the Black and Tans avoided trouble as far as was possible, and were considered in many areas 'not so bad at all'. A Royal Irish Constabulary Inspector was, nevertheless, surprised on a tour of his stations to see the words 'God Save the King. God Bless the Black and Tans', painted in large letters across the front of a public house. On enquiry he found that the publican had assured a group of Black and Tans that he was no 'Shinner', and with a typical access of Irish amiability had added that he had 'a great wish for the Black and Tans'. They thereupon urged him to set a good example and have his good wishes painted up so that all the world would see that he was a decent man. The Black and Tans' sense of fun was often almost as irritating as a reprisal.

There was little to laugh at in Ireland in these days. The daily catalogue of outrages lengthened, and the death-rate rose in March. On what might be called a typical day in the first week, on which nothing out of the ordinary occurred, Volunteers fired on a Black and Tan lorry in Dublin and four civilians were wounded: in an ambush on R.I.C. and military patrols in Leitrim, two Black and Tans and four soldiers were wounded, two of them mortally: the body of an ex-soldier was found in Corry, Roscommon, with the familiar label 'spies and informers beware': an Auxiliary was shot dead while walking out with a girl in Cashel, Tipperary, and the girl wounded: in an ambush on a troop train in Wexford one soldier was killed and one wounded. These were the engagements of one day of war.

On the 7th March the murders of George Clancy, the Mayor of Limerick, and Michael O'Callaghan, the ex-Mayor, caused a fresh outburst of horror and denunciation in almost the whole of the British Press. It was assumed by this time that all murders in Ireland were committed by the Black and Tans or Auxiliaries, although Irish Protestants and ex-soldiers were being shot almost daily as informers, usually without justification. On this occasion there was good reason to believe that the murders had been committed by Irish gunmen. The Mayor and the ex-Mayor had enlisted the aid of a number of priests to help keep order and to prevent outrages in the city. A directive from I.R.A. Headquarters to Clancy, who was a Volunteer Commander, had been intercepted by Dublin Castle's Intelligence. It had asked him peremptorily what he was going to do with four hundred rifles he had been sent. He had done nothing with them. It was not unknown for I.R.A. men to be executed for lack of zeal, and for three months before the murders, Limerick had been so peaceful that the British commander could drive round the city without an escort. Even Michael Collins may have had his doubts about these murders. He ordered an enquiry into them, but added: 'I am, of course, assuming that Black and Tans did it, and it ought consequently to be possible to discover who they were.' For once, however, his agents were not able, or willing, to establish the identity of the culprits.

But in the excited and fevered atmosphere of 1921 there was no time for the nicety of weighing evidence. In one story, popular on Labour platforms, the Black and Tans had captured six Volunteers, had cut the heart out of one, the tongue out of another, the nose off a third and battered in the skull of a fourth. What happened to the other two was not revealed. An attempted rape was reported in Cork; the criminal must have been a member of the Crown Forces, for Mrs. Emmeline Pethwick-Lawrence was able to assure a meeting of the Co-operative Women's Guild that it was a matter of general knowledge that Irishmen were incapable of such an act.

The plain facts were bad enough without these embellishments, but Sinn Fein propagandists were always ready to embroider the truth, even for people who were often more interested in bringing the Government down than in helping Ireland. It all aided the cause. Or did it? A certain hopelessness gripped the contestants on both sides. The I.R.A. could never hope to win, and the Crown Forces were not allowed to. The military had thought that martial law would give them a free hand, but with the moderating influence of Sir John Anderson at Dublin Castle, the powers it conferred were rarely exercised, and conditions in the martial law area were little different from those in other centres of disturbance. The military mind, trained to appreciate a situation and to decide to do this or that, and answer a question 'yes' or 'no', was baffled by the deviousness of politicians who said 'yes' one moment, 'no' the next, and seemed to be doing this and that at the same time. Sir Henry Wilson perfectly illustrated these divergent points of view in a letter to a friend: 'There are two courses and only two, in regard to Ireland,' he wrote. 'One would be to come away which ... would be fatal, and the other is to govern Ireland. Where our politicians fall into the mess in which they are always floundering over Irish affairs is that they will neither come away nor will they govern. They are always attempting some middle course which is fatal to the continued prosperity of Ireland herself and the safety of the Empire.'

Meanwhile, negotiators, notably 'Andy' Cope, were obstinately looking for the middle way to an honourable peace. Newspapers, both in England and in Ireland, reported secret negotiations and hopefully forecast a settlement while violence swelled to a crescendo. In the first week of March Volunteers in Kerry ambushed a military convoy and killed a Brigade Commander, another officer and thirteen soldiers; a fortnight later Tom Barry's Flying Column caught troops who were looking for it, and in three well-planned ambushes near Cork killed over thirty soldiers. General Macready was sufficiently impressed by these two attacks to fear the possibility of a general uprising in the West, and to ask the Government for power to use aircraft to break up rebel concentrations. At the same time Michael Collins was disturbed by reports of local truces arranged between the Crown Forces and the Volunteers, usually through the agency of the priests.

The pattern of resistance was uneven, but the course of events made an immediate peace seem unlikely. On the 14th March six Volunteers were hanged at Mountjoy. One had been sentenced for taking part in the murders of Bloody Sunday, and five had been convicted at a court martial for 'treason and levying war'. There were emotional scenes at the prison. A Black and Tan received Communion with two of the condemned men, and all six shook hands and exchanged greetings with the Auxiliary guards on the way to the scaffold. 'Let my comrades and people outside not mourn for me,' one of them said. 'I am innocent and they have done their worst.' The people outside numbered twenty thousand, and they were kneeling in the rain. Dublin was at a standstill until midday. The shops and post offices were closed, the streets and docks deserted and hotel guests, coming down to breakfast, had to fend for themselves. But this unnatural calm was soon shattered by a street battle between Volunteers and Auxiliaries in which two Volunteers were killed and a number of Auxiliaries, and some civilians, wounded.

In London, Sir Henry Wilson wrote in his diary: 'We must clear out or govern—by which I mean much more drastic steps than we have taken. Sweep up all motors, bicycles, horses, and make the rebels immobile, then close the Post Offices and Banks and then "drive". A foul job for any soldier.' Three days later, on St. Patrick's Day, Sir Hamar Greenwood appeared, jaunty and confident, in the House of Commons with a shamrock in his buttonhole, and Mr. Bonar Law, who looked ill and tired, wearily expressed the hope that 'the beneficent influence of that great Christian and national Saint will permeate Ireland'.

There were, unhappily, few signs of this supernatural guidance in the weeks that followed, and none at all in Ulster, where Catholics had been murdering Protestants and Protestants Catholics since the beginning of the year and where trouble, simmering below the surface, frequently broke out into faction fights and riots. The Irish Republican Army in the North was determined to make the establishment of a separate North Government under the Government of Ireland Act impossible, and sought, by some curious train of reasoning, to emphasise the unity of Ireland by enforcing the boycott of Ulster goods. On the day on which Bonar Law expressed his pious hope, a party of Volunteers occupied a railway station near Belfast, isolated it by cutting the telephone and telegraph wires, and destroyed a number of laden wagons bound for the South. Even the astute de Valera suffered from the delusion that unity could be achieved by a policy of exclusion and in an interview with a correspondent of the Associated Press said:

> The Partition Act is an Act of foreign and hostile assembly. The Irish people as a whole will never accept it. The people even of the Six Counties were never consulted about it in any recognised way. It was designed to perpetuate division and sectional rancour amongst Irishmen. . . . When the elections come, they will prove that Industrial Ulster is not so blind to its own interests as to court being severed from its great market in the agricultural areas in the rest of the island. The boycott of Belfast goods which is now operating is but the opening stage of what will become a complete and absolute exclusion of Belfast goods if the Partition Act is put into effect.

De Valera had a redoubtable opponent in the new champion of the men of the North. Their old leader, Sir Edward Carson, had resigned earlier in the year and had been succeeded by Sir James Craig, at that time Financial Secretary to the Treasury, and later Lord Craigavon. On the occasion of this appointment, Sir Edward Carson succinctly defined Ulster's political standpoint: 'Ulster may be won by argument,' he said. 'Ulster may be won by a sincere profession of the same ideals of loyalty and attachment to the Throne and Constitution, and Ulster may be won by a pride in Empire and an acceptance of the glorious principles which have made our country great throughout the world. But Ulster will never be coerced.' Sir James Craig was eager to put the Government of Ireland Act into operation as soon as possible. He knew the ways of Westminster and the wiles of Lloyd George, and feared that the Government might yet try to extricate itself from its difficulties in the South by sacrificing the interests of the North. 'You have done me the honour to elect me as your leader,' he told his supporters, 'and I mean to lead.' He urged on them the necessity for resolution, and for speed, and warned them: 'The British Government will let us down tomorrow if they can get the smallest advantage out of it.'

He had every reason for his fears when he saw what happened to the Southern Unionists. On the 24th March the Privy Council met in London to fix the 'appointed days' for bringing the Government of Ireland, or 'Partition', Act into operation. Lord Edmund Talbot, later Lord Fitzalan, was designated Lord French's successor as Viceroy. He was by birth a Howard, and therefore a member of England's premier Roman Catholic family. His appointment was meant to conciliate Sinn Fein, whose opinion was summed up by a spokesman who declared that a Catholic hangman would be as welcome. The 19th April was chosen as the date on which the Government would issue the necessary Orders in Council, and the 3rd May the date on which the Act would come into force, and arrangements for a general election be made. The Southern Unionists, the loyal and unwavering supporters of the Government, were aghast and brought what pressure they could to bear to prevent the holding of elections until conditions were more settled. They pointed out that for any man to stand against Sinn Fein, or even vote against it, in the condition of the country as it was, would be more than his life was worth. Lloyd George and Sir Hamar Greenwood stood firm and declared, to the mystification and baffled rage of their supporters in Ireland, that they would not be deflected from their purpose by the 'murder gangs'. 'The Chief Secretary had visions of candidates standing in opposition to Sinn Fein,' General Macready reported. 'I had no doubts on the subject whatsoever, nor had any of those who lived in the country and were in touch with what was going on.'

The prospect of Home Rule, on terms which the North had accepted grudgingly and the South rejected entirely, sharpened rather than diminished resistance. On the 30th March de Valera heartened the Volunteers by declaring that the Dáil assumed responsibility for their actions. In an interview with an American correspondent he said:

> ...From the Irish Volunteers we fashioned the Irish Republican Army to be the military arm of the Government. This army is, therefore, a regular State force, under the civil control of the elected representatives, under organisation and a discipline imposed by these representatives. The Government is, therefore, responsible for the actions of this army. . . .

His cautious attitude to the war had caused some misgiving to the I.R.A. die-hards, but this retrospective recognition vindicated him in their eyes, and his defence of ambushes gave heart to the Flying Columns. He described the Crown Forces as invaders and said:

> ... Protected by the most modern war appliances, they swoop down upon us and kill and burn and loot

and outrage—why should it be wrong for us to see that they will not do these things with impunity? If they may use their tanks and steel-armoured cars, why should we hesitate to use the cover of stone walls and ditches? Why should the element of surprise be denied to us? . . . If German forces had landed in England during the recent war, would it have been wrong for Englishmen to surprise them . . . to harass their invader by every means in their power? If not wrong for Englishmen, why wrong for us?

Nearly every day, somewhere in the 30,000 square miles of Ireland, soldiers and police were ambushed, a Volunteer or an informer was taken out and shot, and civilians were wounded in shooting affrays started by one side or another. The Volunteers were hard pressed. Colonel Winter, or 'the Holy Terror' as the I.R.A. knew him, had set up an Intelligence network in Dublin Castle that was beginning to worry Michael Collins, who was often known as 'the Laughing Boy'. Winter had two Volunteer Commandants on his pay roll in Cork, and his agents were enrolling others all over the country. £500, and the offer of a free passage out of the country to any part of the world he liked in the event of discovery, was the standard offer for an I.R.A. informant. Few of these who were discovered lived to avail themselves of this offer.

Winter's 'Raid Bureau' examined all captured documents and made epitomes, some of them running to six hundred pages. A 'rogues' gallery' of wanted men was also built up by a photographic section, but the documents were the most valuable source of information, and revealed the location of arms dumps, lists of Volunteers, the time and place of intended attacks, the movement of wanted men, and even the names of all but one of Michael Collins' agents among the detectives in Dublin Castle. This one exception had been enrolled in the British Secret Service and was a valuable source of information to Collins to the end. Nevertheless, 'the Holy Terror' was harassing 'the Laughing Boy', who tried to dispose of his adversary by an amateurish bomb plot and put £1,000 price on his head—a poor compliment Winter thought when Collins himself and Dan Breen were valued at £10,000 dead or alive. In this duel, Michael Collins' Intelligence Office in Mespil Road was discovered, and he himself was very nearly caught. His Finance Ministry Offices, in Mary Street, were raided a few weeks later and he realised with a sinking heart that one of his associates was a traitor. Batt O'Connor, who specialised in building secret rooms and cupboards in houses likely to be raided, records the following exchange between Collins and himself on this occasion.

'Batt,' he said, 'they will get me now in a fortnight.'

'Arrah! Michael, not at all. Sure isn't God Almighty protecting you?'

'Ah it is different this time. I am being given away from the inside, and those who know about Mary Street know everything else about me.'

It was true enough, but he was still able to walk or cycle round Dublin unrecognised, and to bluff his way past search parties and patrols to the end. The Crown Forces often did not realise when they had made an important capture. Ernie O'Malley, one of the I.R.A.'s best known and most capable commanders, had, for example, been in Kilmainham Gaol for three months without being recognised by the Intelligence Officers who tortured him before he escaped in the middle of February. Séan McKeon, another chivalrous and courageous guerilla commander, was less lucky. He was recognised on a visit to Dublin and trailed to his home, where he was arrested after a gun battle in which he killed a District Inspector of the Royal Irish Constabulary. It was becoming more difficult to slip through the net.

During one raid, on the 26th March, the offices of *The Irish Bulletin*, the weekly Roneoed Sinn Fein news sheet, was discovered, and the Roneo, the typewriter and its distribution list were taken to Dublin Castle. A resourceful member of General Tudor's staff, W. Y. Darling, later Sir William Darling, C.B.E., M.C., D.L., J.P., M.P., and Lord Provost of Edinburgh, decided to write, print and distribute a bogus issue. He modelled the style carefully on the original and an extract reads:

> The tactics of the Republican Forces have been masterly in handling the situation created by the English Government in flooding Ireland with ex-soldiers in the uniform of police. In no single recorded case have the Republican Forces attacked a single policeman with the odds less than six to one. By this strategic handling of all combats victory has invariably rested with the Republicans. Science in war, as practised by the young men of Ireland, has staggered humanity—and it will be a long time ere humanity recovers from the blow.

This bogus *Irish Bulletin* went for some weeks, to the same addresses as the genuine article, and served to blunt the edge of Sinn Fein's skilfully conducted propaganda. Some of the I.R.A.'s excesses in the increasingly savage temper of these days also shocked many of the staunchest friends of the Irish cause. On the 14th April, for example, Sir Arthur Vicars, formerly Ulster King at Arms, was taken out of his home in Listowel and shot. The label tied round his neck read: 'Spy. Informers beware. I.R.A. never forgets.' This execution was described by *The Manchester Guardian*, which had consistently opposed the Government's policy in Ireland, as:

> ... one of the most horrible in the black recent records of crime and counter-crime in Ireland. For a crowd of armed men to attack an unarmed man in a lonely house, take him out of bed and jointly murder him,

they must have debauched their minds with the base casuistry of a 'state of war' to an extent which makes them a curse to any cause they pretend to honour. Nothing honourable in public affairs can spring from anyone's personal dishonour, and anyone, be he Sinn Feiner or anti-Sinn Feiner, who take a part in one of these dastard 'executions' writes himself down a leper for whom no brave and pure cause has a place in its service. There is nothing as yet that a court would call proof of the authorship of this particular abomination. A tag attached to the corpse is said to boast it for the 'Irish Republican Army'. It may be a genuine brag; it is a loathsome one, if so; or it may be the trick of some enemy of the alleged braggarts. We cannot know; in either case the crime, like all of its kind, is an act of the foulest treason to any cause to which those guilty of it profess loyalty.

Sinn Fein propagandists in London were puzzled by this outburst. This murder was no worse than many others that had gone unnoticed. The popular Press used the occasion to resurrect the story of the theft of Irish Crown Jewels from Dublin Castle in 1907. This successful coup, one of the most intriguing in the history of burglary, had caused the resignation of Sir Arthur Vicars, who, as Ulster King at Arms, had been nominally responsible for the safeguarding of the jewels which were never recovered. But the press of current events left little space for Irish reminiscences. Between the 10th and the 23rd April, eighteen members of the R.I.C. and two soldiers were killed. On the 15th four Volunteers ambushed a Major McKinnon on Tralee golfcourse. He was an efficient and greatly feared Auxiliary Commander whom they had been trying to kill for months. Such an exploit was naturally enshrined in a ballad, the first two verses of which read:

Attend again, brave comrades
While I retell the tale,
In a few simple verses
Of a despot's bloody trail;
From cursed England's reeking shores
He came to mow us down,
And laughed to scorn a voice that warned
'Don't go to Tralee Town'.

Now this grim British Major
Had planned to crush Sinn Fein,
To shoot and loot and play once more
The good old Empire game;
But rebels of *The Kingdom* swore
Our dear old land to free,
And shot the tyrant Major
In the golf links at Tralee.

On the next day a young woman, Kitty Carrol, sole
support of an aged father and mother as well as of an
invalid brother, was dragged from her home by Volunteers
and shot as a spy. This murder went unsung, but was fully
reported, to the distress of Sinn Fein propagandists. On
the 19th April a party of Auxiliary cadets shot up some
Black and Tans by mistake in a raid on the Shannon View
Hotel, Castle Connell. Two Auxiliaries and one Black and
Tan were killed before they combined forces to terrorise
the guests, murder the landlord and wreck the bar with
hand grenades. Lord Parmoor's brother, who had gone
to Ireland for a fishing holiday, was one of the guests; he
wrote a letter, which was read a few days later to a shocked
and attentive House of Lords. On the same day Black and
Tans ran amok in Tralee and burned a newspaper office
and several shops and houses. On the 27th District Inspector
Gilbert Potter, of the R.I.C., was shot as a reprisal for the
execution of a Republican. 'I never felt more sorry in my

life at having to carry out such an unpleasant task,' Dan Breen wrote. 'We discussed the matter from every aspect but agreed we had no alternative. Potter was a kind and cultured gentleman and a brave officer. Before he was executed he gave us a diary, a signet ring and a gold watch with the request we should return them to his wife.'

On both sides there was a growing number of men who were prepared to shoot somebody rather than nobody. On the day after Potter's death, Major Compton Smith, D.S.O., of the Royal Welsh Fusiliers was also executed as a hostage. He was, according to Pieras Beaslai, the I.R.A. Director of Publicity, 'a man of amiable and estimable character who had done nothing unworthy against us. Unfortunately in these dreadful times, this generous and kindly gentleman had to suffer for the atrocities of the "Forces of the Crown".' This victim lent some dignity to the squalid episode by his last letter to his wife in which he wrote: 'I am to be shot in an hour's time. Dearest, your husband will die with your name on his lips, your face before his eyes, and he will die like an Englishman and a soldier. I leave my cigarette case to the Regiment, my medals to my Father, and my watch to the officer who is to execute me, because I believe him to be a gentleman and to mark the fact that I bear him no malice for carrying out what he sincerely believes to be his duty.'

In 1922, in the debate in the Dáil on the Anglo-Irish Treaty, Richard Mulcahy argued against a renewal of the war, because it would put on Ireland 'the responsibility of killing in self-defence the Compton Smiths of England'.

Collins was disturbed by the bad propaganda effect of some of these executions, and, as in the case of Mrs. Lindsay, said he would have used his influence to stop the shooting of Major Compton Smith if he had known about it. The Englishman, Erskine Childers, who had been appointed the Dáil's Director of Publicity, was also worried and wrote to Collins: 'Shall we say, (a) the execution of women spies is forbidden, and that Kitty Carrol was not killed by the I.R.A.? Or (b) Kitty Carrol was killed in contravention of orders by the I.R.A., and that (c) Mrs. Lindsay is now in prison for giving information to the enemy, leading to the death of three of the I.R.A.?' Mrs. Lindsay had been dead for some weeks when he wrote this letter, but propagandists are no more on their oath than are the composers of epitaphs. 'In Erskine Childers the Republic had the advocate of genius,' Dorothy Macardle observed in her history, *The Irish Republic*. Arthur Griffith, often charged by Irishmen with being a Welshman, called him 'that damned Englishman'. He had certainly done good work for Ireland in the English press, where the I.R.A. was continuing the struggle. I.R.A. activities, strangely, did little to alienate sympathy for the Irish cause, and created neither general interest nor hostility.

A plot to blow up bridges in Glasgow was discovered and two Volunteers were arrested at the beginning of April. On the 3rd April three hotels, a large café and a warehouse were set on fire in Manchester, and a policeman was shot at and wounded, and a man killed in a raid on an Irish club. Groups of armed and masked Volunteers made a number of raids on the homes of Black and Tans and Auxiliaries in London and Liverpool, and in some cases managed to set them on fire. Volunteers also booked rooms in hotels and set them alight before leaving. A renegade I.R.A. man, whom Colonel Winter had sent over from Ireland as an agent to penetrate the organisation in England, was found shot dead on Ashford Manor Golf Course. The I.R.A. campaign was reproducing itself in miniature in the territory of the Saxon oppressor. A campaign of shop window smashing, which started in London and rapidly spread over the country, was greeted in Dublin as another sign that the war was being carried to the enemy, but the I.R.A. commanders in England claimed that this was the work of unknown maniacs. They also disclaimed responsi-

40. Irishwomen, in general, showed more enthusiasm for the republican cause than the men. They used both private persuasion and public demonstration to prick the consciences of faint-hearts and neutrals.

41. Poignant scenes attended executions. The Irish despatched one another with less ceremony in the civil war, when seventy-seven republicans were executed between November, 1922 and May, 1923.

42. Outside Mountjoy: Miss Barry Delaney, Madame Maude MacBride, who was one of the most attractive features of what Dublin Castle officials called 'the Republican Scenic Railway', and the redoubtable Miss Annie MacSwiney, sister of the Lord Mayor of Cork.

43. Behind the Wire: Nearly five thousand republicans had been incarcerated in internment camps by the early summer of 1921. Conditions were not severe. Many were glad to he out of the struggle.

bility for the people who were pouring pitch and acid into pillar boxes in Manchester, Liverpool and Glasgow. These minor outrages served to emphasise the futility, and even idiocy, of a conflict that seemed to be governed neither by principle nor expediency.

The agitation for peace was intensified in the Spring of 1921. 'We must make peace some time. Why not now?' was the question Lord Henry Cavendish-Bentinck asked the country in a campaign waged by his Peace with Ireland Council. Mr. Asquith demanded the disbandment of the Black and Tans, and provoked another stormy scene in the House of Commons. In the Cabinet, Sir Austen Chamberlain, the leader of the Conservative Party, Winston Churchill and others advocated a policy defined by Lord Birkenhead, the Lord Chancellor, as 'the fairest offer combined with the most drastic threats'. Lloyd George was anxious for peace but felt, with some reason, that he was being asked to surrender to 'murder gangs'. He told Lord Riddell: 'The question is whether I can see Michael Collins. The question is whether the British people would be willing for me to negotiate with a band of murderers.' But the majority of the British people was, by this time, in no mood to object to any talks that might lead to a settlement.

At the beginning of April a group of Protestant and Nonconformist ministers, headed by the Bishop of Chelmsford, told Lloyd George in a letter that his policy in Ireland was 'causing grave unrest throughout the Empire', and that it was exposing the country 'to the hostile criticism of even the most friendly nations of the world' and called for a truce. In the course of a lengthy and well-argued reply, Lloyd George admitted, but did not condone, the excesses of the Black and Tans and Auxiliaries. 'I venture to believe', he wrote, 'that when the history of the past nine months comes to be written, and the authentic acts of misconduct can be disentangled from the vastly greater mass of reckless and lying accusations, the general record of patience and forbearance displayed, by the Auxiliaries as well as by the ordinary Constabulary, will command not the condemnation, but the admiration of posterity.' He agreed that the follies of past governments had created the present conditions, but asked a question that worried many Sinn Feiners when he wrote:

... I do not contest Sinn Fein's right to its opinions and aspirations, and I have never done so. But what amazes me is that a body of responsible men, eminent leaders of the Church, should state publicly that Sinn Fein has some kind of justification for murdering innocent men in cold blood, because its novel and extravagant political ideals have been denied.

Where does the doctrine end? There is a small but vigorous Communist Party in these islands, which bitterly and with the most intense conviction believes that it ought to overthrow democratic institutions and seize power by force and violence, because of the manner in which they consider the ruling classes of the past, the aristocracy and the owners of capital, oppressed and exploited the poor. Are the Communists, because of the sufferings and grievances of the working classes and the sincerity of their own industrial ideals, to be justified in employing murder and assassination to achieve these ends?

It was a good point that had been obscured by the clamour of propaganda. The Communist Party of Great Britain later had some difficulty with ex-I.R.A. men who joined their ranks and had to be dissuaded from attempts to advance the cause by assassinating selected Cabinet Ministers and Trades Union leaders. On the question of peace terms, Lloyd George was uncompromising, and wrote:

... So long, therefore, as Sinn Fein Ireland demands a republic and refuses to accept loyally membership of the British Commonwealth, coupled with Home Rule which is compatible with conceding to Ulster the same rights as it claims for itself, the present evils will continue. I do not wish anybody to be under any misunderstanding on that point.

Lloyd George was as much restricted by what de Valera called 'the strait-jacket of the republic' as were the leaders of Sinn Fein. The members of the Opposition, who so roundly abused him, were no more ready to grant the demand for complete independence than he was. Few Englishmen could take seriously the claim that Ireland, which had been a part of the United Kingdom for some centuries, could be a separate and independent country, either on the grounds of common sense or of strategy. The majority of Sinn Fein members, who were perfectly prepared to accept Dominion status, as they proved in the voting on the Treaty in 1922, felt it impossible to retreat from the premature, and ill-advised, declaration of a Republic in 1918. In an attempt to break the deadlock, Lord Derby went to Dublin, where he stayed at the Gresham Hotel under the name of Mr. Edwards. He saw de Valera, as an unofficial emissary, to sound his opinions on the granting of a form of Dominion status to Ireland. De Valera insisted that no settlement was possible unless Ireland's rights were fully recognised. Lord Derby returned to London to report to Lloyd George, and wrote to de Valera to ask whether he insisted on the principle of full independence being conceded before negotiations began. On the 26th April, de Valera countered with a question for the Prime Minister: 'Will he not consent to meet one or any representatives of the (Irish) Government unless the principle of complete independence be first surrendered by us?'

This question was not immediately answered, but hopes for peace ran high. The Irish Dominion League made proposals which attracted many Sinn Feiners and alarmed the Republican extremists. Its president was Sir Horace Plunkett, who had pioneered the Irish Agricultural Co-operatives, which had suffered damage estimated as over £250,000 since the arrival of the Black and Tans. Cardinal Logue lent the Dominion League the support of the Hierarchy, by implication, when he said, on the 30th April: 'I know for a fact that if people in Ireland abandon crime they can obtain everything that is necessary for the country. An Irish Republic they will never have, so long as England has a man to fight.' On the same day, five Cork men who had been condemned to death, were reprieved—a hopeful sign, it seemed, of a conciliatory policy—and the British Government issued its casualty figures to date, in what many optimistically believed to be a final account. They were: 291 police and 102 soldiers killed and 485 police and 235 soldiers wounded.

On the 2nd May, J. J. Farrell, an ex-Lord Mayor of Dublin, said that he had received proposals for peace from a representative of the British Government. This was denied by Sir Austen Chamberlain in the House of Commons on the next day, but Lloyd George told Martin Glynn, an ex-Governor of the State of New York, that he was pre-pared to meet de Valera, or any other Irish leaders, without conditions of any sort. On the 5th May de Valera and Sir James Craig, the Ulster leader, met in Dublin, and excited the expectations of an Ireland that would be both peaceful and united. But both men had been led by the intermediaries to believe that the other had asked for the meeting, and Sir James Craig was able to assure his followers on his return to the North, that Ulster, 'having reached the limit of concession, no further discussion will be entered into'. On the 11th May de Valera, who had been informed of the Lloyd George conversation with Martin Glynn, said in an interview:

If Mr. Lloyd George makes this statement in public I shall give him a public reply. The fundamental question at issue between the two countries is the question of Ireland's right to choose freely and independently her own government and political institutions at home and her relationships with foreign nations as well. This independent right may as well be acknowledged first as last, for there can never be a settlement as long as it is denied.

Lloyd George, who was under pressure from the die-hard Conservatives in his increasingly shaky Coalition Government, was not prepared to make the public offer that de Valera both wanted and needed if he was to maintain his own position in the Dáil. Lloyd George certainly could not risk a public rebuff and he reverted instead to his idea of arranging a truce, in which passions might cool and talking become possible, at least for the period of the General Election under the Government of Ireland Act, which had been fixed for the 17th May in the South and the 24th May in the North. Sir Henry Wilson opposed this idea and told the Prime Minister: 'We are having more success than usual in killing rebels and now is the time to reinforce and not to parley.'

Some of Sir Henry's compatriots, on the other side, thought on similar lines. *An t-Oglac* told the Volunteers: 'One of the usual symptoms of the enemy's suffering "cold feet" is the circulation by him of stories of "peace moves". It is a desperate resort when things are going badly for him . . . .For us the one order, the great and serious duty of the moment is: "Get on with the war".'

Peace was round the corner, but it was a dangerous and difficult corner to negotiate.

CHAPTER TWELVE

The Truce at Last

NOMINATION DAY for the General Election under the Government of Ireland Act was the 13th May, 1921. 'Where except in Ireland, or possibly in a South American Republic,' General Macready wrote, 'could open rebellion, martial law, peace proposals and a General Election be all running side by side at one and the same time? And yet no Irishman or politician seemed to think anything funny about it! Perhaps the simple minded soldier is easily amused, and certainly we were over in Ireland.' But the excitements and humours of the hustings were denied to the electors in the Twenty-six Counties in the South, where all the candidates were returned unopposed—a hundred and twenty-four for Sinn Fein, and four University Unionists for Trinity College, Dublin. All but a dozen of the Sinn Fein members had served prison sentences, and some, notably Arthur Griffith, Countess Markievicz and Séan McKeon, who was being held on a charge of murder, but who was released after the Truce to play a prominent part in the affairs of the Republic, were still in prison. A single-party list is not regarded these days as an impressive indication of the people's will, but at least the Irish electors in the South were not obliged to go to the polls in the now recognised authoritarian manner, and no votes were cast.

The election was known in Ireland as the 'Partition Election' and the leaders of the old Nationalist Parliamentary Party, although politically opposed to Sinn Fein, had decided not to split the anti-partition vote. A more

[198]

formidable opponent, the Irish Labour Party, which a year before had been the dominant force in the struggle for independence with its own socialist programme, contented itself with 'calling upon all workers, North and South, to demonstrate their loyalty to Ireland and freedom by voting only for those candidates who stand for the ownership and government of Ireland by the people of Ireland', without putting up candidates pledged to secure that end. Thus, the party founded by James Connolly, who had been the first to declare for a socialist republic, had no say, either in the negotiations for a settlement, or in the debates on the Treaty which preceded the Civil War. Later in the year, only a fortnight after the Truce on the 11th July, but still too late, Cathal O'Shannon, one of the ablest and most spirited of Labour leaders, declared that 'labour is not tied to the tail of Dáil Eireann, or to the tail of the Irish Republican Army, because we might at any moment have to fight them and get as clear of them as we had of the British Army'. But when the fight came, the gombeen men were in full control.

It is tempting to speculate how different the history of Ireland might have been if Labour had contested the election with a socialist programme, or even how much bloodshed and destruction have been spared the country if the British Government had offered Ireland the terms in December, 1918, which were finally agreed, three years later, in December, 1921. De Valera's often repeated claim that the Irish people had voted for a Republic in 1918 was adroit political jugglery, but it was never true, and the supposedly Republican members of the Dáil finally proved its falsity when, in spite of Black and Tans, Auxiliaries, murders, executions, arson, recriminations and memory of ancient wrongs, they voted, on the 7th January, 1922, for Dominion status by a majority of sixty-four to fifty-seven.

But these events lay in the future, and the Truce was still two months away. The elections in the Six Counties in the

North were more eventful. 'The Union Jack must sweep the polls,' Sir James Craig said in his eve-of-poll address on the 23rd May. 'The eyes of our friends throughout the Empire are upon us. Let them see that we are as determined as they to uphold the cause of loyalty.' Polling day was also Empire Day and Belfast was festooned with Union Jacks. Enthusiastic Orangemen had even, in places, painted the pavements red, white and blue. Sir Edward Carson told the electors, in a pre-electoral message, that 'Ulster must be saved from the assassin vote'. In a rival message, de Valera urged them to 'vote tomorrow against war with your fellow countrymen. Vote that brother's hand may not have to be raised against brother's. Vote so that there may be an end to boycott and retaliation, to partition, disunion and ruin. Orange and Green together can command the future. Ireland one is Ireland peaceful, prosperous and happy. Vote for it.'

In the Six Counties of Ulster, brother's hand had been raised more than once against brother's in 1921. Flying Columns of the I.R.A. had been raiding R.I.C. barracks and also farms belonging to Unionists, two of whom had been killed; Volunteers had bombed the Unionist Club in Belfast and Orangemen had taken young men, suspected of being 'Shinners', and had shot them. Ambushes of the police were almost as common as in the South, though less effective. During the election campaign Orange mobs had wrecked Labour and Sinn Fein offices, sometimes with the help of Ulster Special Constables who were often little more than licensed thugs. In outlying districts the I.R.A. blew up bridges and scattered the roads with nails in a forlorn attempt to stop Unionist communities getting to the polls. The military and police were out in force on polling day, and though there was some rioting, there was no serious incident by Ulster standards. Ninety per cent of the electorate voted, a very high proportion, and they got to and from the polling booths without loss of life or limb.

The issue was Partition or not. The result showed that the antipathy of Ulstermen to the idea of being ruled by a government in the Catholic South was, however misguided, not a myth manufactured in Westminster. Of the fifty-two seats, the Unionists won forty, the Nationalists six, and Sinn Fein six. De Valera, Michael Collins and Arthur Griffith were three of the successful Sinn Fein candidates. But the Unionist victory was not complete. Fermanagh and Tyrone returned four Unionists, three Sinn Feiners and one Nationalist, and the votes showed an anti-Partition majority of over seven thousand. These two counties were, and still are, a source of constant trouble to the Government of Northern Ireland.

The results of the election in the North were a severe disappointment to Sinn Fein. Even the Unionists had not expected so large a victory, and some had privately expected defeat. The I.R.A. in the South had not been idly awaiting the election results in the North since the unopposed electoral success of Sinn Fein on the 13th May, and they did not relax their efforts during the Whitsun week-end that started on the following day. On Friday, while others went to the races or to the seaside, they shot a District Inspector and a woman friend who were starting off on a motoring holiday; on the Saturday they killed over a dozen soldiers and police. Twenty Galway Volunteers caught another District Inspector, his wife and an army officer who were returning from a tennis party on Whit-Sunday and killed them, and as a reprisal the Royal Irish Constabulary burned houses over a wide area. Michael Collins tried to organise the escape of Séan McKeon from Mountjoy Gaol on the same day, but his luck had deserted him since the 'Holy Terror', Winter, had tightened up security. This, however, was a minor reverse, and the holiday week-end bag included twenty dead soldiers and police who had been caught in ambushes.

The Daily News declared that it had been a 'black Whitsun' in Ireland, and Dublin Castle announced that the casualties for the week ending the 16th May were 'the highest since the Rebellion of 1916'. The reprisals which followed these attacks stimulated another outburst of protest in the Press, on public platforms, and even from Buckingham Palace. 'The King does ask himself and he asks you if this policy of reprisals is to be continued,' Lord Stamfordham, the King's Private Secretary, wrote to Sir Hamar Greenwood, 'and, if so, to where will it lead Ireland and us all? It seems to His Majesty that in punishing the guilty we are inflicting punishment no less severe upon the innocent.' Few people believed that the Government's policy would bring peace to Ireland, and Volunteers fortified the conviction by making another series of attacks on the homes of Black and Tans and Auxiliaries in London, in the course of which they gave the mother of one a flesh wound in the thigh and the father of another a mortal wound in the stomach. London police began rounding up Irishmen and deporting them to Ireland. Some of them had earlier been rounded up in Ireland and deported to England.

An t-Oglach was constantly urging its readers that 'even where there is no opportunity for bringing off ambushes or big coups there are still a hundred ways of harassing the enemy and inflicting moral and material damage and loss upon him'. It often quoted useful stratagems that had been tried out in the field, such as that sent in by a Volunteer from Longford. He wrote: 'I placed a Republican Flag out of a chimney *with grenade attached.* On going up for same one or two were badly got and also some more on the ground.' But such actions, useful as they were, and even successful ambushes, where it was possible to inflict casualties at little risk and at not more than ten yards range, or the bold execution of the porter of the Wicklow Hotel in the middle of Dublin as a spy, in broad daylight, all somehow seemed to miss the glory and panache that should attach to heroes in a War of Independence.

The leading figures of the Irish Republican Army had, for some time, been considering some action that would capture the imagination of the world. De Valera had suggested an attack on the Auxiliary Headquarters in Beggars Bush Barracks in Dublin, but a preliminary reconnaissance showed this venture to be difficult, if not impossible, to execute. De Valera's alternative suggestion was to burn the Custom House. This fine eighteenth-century building housed the offices of the Local Government Board as well as the Inland Revenue. It was a convenient symbol of British oppression and had the additional advantage of not being considered important enough to be guarded. It was adopted as the objective for what was to be the Irish Republic Army's most famous victory, in which more Volunteers were engaged than in any other.

For some weeks the Volunteers of the Dublin Brigade had been preparing a type of operation at which they often excelled. They secured plans of the building, and a battalion commander walked all over it, disguised as a messenger, to reconnoitre. Others investigated the possibilities of immobilising the fire stations long enough for the fire to take hold, and of cutting the telephone wires to the building. The I.R.A.'s Director of Supplies sent out scouts to find the best sources for the considerable quantity of cotton waste and paraffin needed for so ambitious an attempt at arson. It was difficult to maintain complete security with so many Volunteers involved, and Sir Henry Robinson, the Chairman of the Local Government Board, heard rumours that an attack on the Custom House was imminent. He asked Dublin Castle to provide a military or police guard, but his request was ignored. The Dublin Castle Intelligence Service knew that some important operation was being prepared by the I.R.A., but discounted, as a bluff, the suggestion that it was to be no more than a raid on the headquarters of the Local Government Board and the Inland Revenue.

The attack on the 25th May thus took the Castle completely by surprise. At 12.55 p.m. Volunteers of the Third and Fourth Battalions of the Dublin Brigade, I.R.A., occupied the fire stations: engineers of the Fifth Battalion cut the communications between the Custom House and the outside world: the First Battalion took up positions round the building to provide protective pickets, while the Second Battalion, fortified by Collins' 'Squad', burned the building. The incendiarists, dressed as workmen, carried tons of paraffin through the three entrances. Most of the staff were at lunch and the Volunteers were able to take up their positions according to a pre-arranged plan without exciting suspicion. Armed Volunteers entered the offices and conducted the startled men and women clerks at pistol point to the stone passages on the ground floor, where they were kept under guard while the good work went on. The Volunteers piled all the furniture, files and papers in a heap in every office, soaked them in paraffin and set them alight. They were about to leave when they were horrified to hear shooting outside.

While they had been busy setting the building on fire, a Dublin Metropolitan Policeman heard that the 'Shinners' were raiding the building as he rode by on his bicycle at one o'clock, and had made all speed to the Castle. He sprinted into the Lower Castle Yard, where he found a party of seventeen Auxiliaries about to sit down to lunch. They jumped into their Crossley tender, and within five minutes were engaging the Volunteer pickets, whom they quickly dispersed. They next turned their attention to the building. A hundred and twenty Volunteers were trapped with their temporary prisoners inside the Custom House, and whenever they opened the iron doors of the building to look out they were met with accurate fire from the dreaded Auxiliaries. The flames had taken hold and the building was beginning to fill with smoke. Some of the younger Volunteers, who had never been in action before, panicked, and ran up and down the passages, crying and swearing, and some called piteously to their Commanders: 'You got us into this and you've got to get us out of it.' Even the veteran members of the 'Squad', expert executioners though they were, had little experience of meeting resistance.

It was soon over. The Auxiliaries stormed the building. About forty Volunteers broke through and escaped in the confusion, and the rest surrendered. The military arrived and rounded up the officials, clerks and prisoners. It was not easy, at first, to tell which was which, for the Volunteers threw away their arms and claimed to be members of the Local Government Board. They were all taken under guard to shelter under a wall outside, where the Assistant Secretary of the Board separated the sheep from the goats.

One office that was missed by the Volunteers was that of Sir George Vanston, the Board's Legal Adviser, who had been angrily ringing for a messenger to bring him some lunch. He was stone deaf and had heard nothing. An officer arrested him as he came out of his office to see what had gone wrong with the messenger service. Although he protested that he was the Legal Adviser to the Board, the officer firmly escorted him out of the burning building to be identified. As he recovered from the shock of his arrest, Sir George noticed that all was not as it should be with the Custom House and shouted at the officer: 'Has there been some firing going on?' Later, Vanston said: 'I thought he looked queerly at me, but anyway he pushed me out into the street and let me go.' The Custom House adventure of the Assistant Secretary, who had identified the prisoners, ended less happily. He was warned, the next day, that the I.R.A. was after him and was advised to take a holiday in England. He went, but not to safety, for on his arrival a Scotland Yard officer told him that, according to police information, he was being followed. He was warned that he must keep constantly on the move and never sleep for two nights in any one place, and abandon, for ever, any thought of returning to Ireland. This unhappy civil servant, who was highly strung and excitable by nature, sold his house at a loss, gave up his appointment and suffered a nervous breakdown. He was, perhaps, the oddest casualty in any war, even though he was later compensated by the Treasury with a retirement allowance.

The Custom House burned for a week and the inside was gutted. The Dublin Brigade of the I.R.A. had achieved its object, but at the cost of five dead, many wounded and eighty prisoners. Four Auxiliaries were also wounded in this action which showed, *An t-Oglach* told its readers: 'The relentless determination of the Government and soldiers of the Irish Republic to wage warfare on every portion of the machinery of alien robbery and violence. . . . The headquarters from which the enemy carried on his campaign of interference with the legal administration of the Local Government of Ireland under Dáil Eireann, the headquarters of the machinery by which he raised a large amount of taxation from the people of Ireland have "gone west".' The claim was a little exaggerated. The Local Government Board was able to resume its almost non-existent labours at ten o'clock next morning in other offices, but the Inland Revenue records had all been destroyed. The tax collectors were, however, not banished from the building for ever. The Irish Government restored the Custom House after the Anglo-Irish Treaty and it became the headquarters of the Irish Revenue Commissioners.

The burning of the Custom House was so obviously futile as a military operation that it did have a certain symbolic impressiveness, and it fortified the growing conviction in Ireland and in England that there was no point in continuing a struggle which seemed more lunatic every day. But this was not the opinion of Sir Hamar Greenwood who said, the day after burning: 'The Government will go on with patience and courage until the last revolver is plucked out of the hands of the last assassin in

Ireland.' That afternoon he proposed to the Cabinet that the whole of the South should be put under martial law on the 12th July, if the Sinn Fein members had not by then accepted the limited Home Rule granted by the Government of Ireland Act, and started their Parliament on the 28th June. The Cabinet, which for months had been vacillating between a policy of conciliation and of coercion, finally agreed to this measure, and to a substantial reinforcement of the forces in Ireland. One consideration which had prevented the earlier despatch of more troops to Ireland had been the revolutionary possibilities of a triple strike by miners, railwaymen and transport workers. The miners had finally struck alone on the 31st March, but the threat of the triple strike still existed. J. H. Thomas, the railwaymen's leader, told Lloyd George, on the 1st April: 'Jesus Christ himself could not now stop this revolutionary movement', but promised to do his human best to avoid the extension of the strike with the help of Ernest Bevin who was then serving his apprenticeship to high office as an official of the Dock, Wharf, Riverside and General Workers' Union. Four battalions were withdrawn from Ireland during the first week of April, and a further six held ready for immediate despatch to England; but by the 15th the industrial position had improved to such an extent, from the Government's point of view, that J. H. Thomas asked the Government to provide troops to protect railwaymen against the embittered miners. The four battalions withdrawn were returned to Ireland early in May, and other troops were promised as soon as the miners met with their inevitable defeat.

The Cabinet decision to reinforce Ireland leaked into the Press and rallied the opponents of the Government policy to further efforts. 'The Military pull in Ireland is strong,' *The Manchester Guardian* commented, 'and the position is critical.' On the 1st June Sir Hamar Greenwood stood up to the heaviest assault yet launched against him in the House

of Commons. Members of all parties criticised the futility
and inhumanity of the policy of reprisals. Colonel Guinness
read a letter from a Southern Loyalist: 'If the military
reprisals go on there will be no loyalist houses left. The
Government cannot protect anyone,' and asked: 'How can
you quell a rebellion by burning a farmer's house worth
£800 when he can burn a landlord's mansion worth
£20,000?' Lord Winterton urged that if there had to be
military action in Ireland it should be short and sharp,
and that a continuation of guerilla warfare was intolerable.
Ramsay MacDonald, the leader of the Labour Party, called
for a complete reversal of the Government's policy—a
procedure at which he later became expert as the first
Labour Prime Minister. No member spoke in favour of
reprisals, and Sir Hamar Greenwood was, for the first time,
on the defensive and promised to review the policy, and to
put the points raised in the debate to General Macready.

Meanwhile, the I.R.A. campaign was becoming desperate and intense. Six soldiers were killed and twenty-one
wounded by a mine at Youghal in Cork on the last day of
May, and two District Inspectors and thirteen members of
the R.I.C. were killed and twenty-one wounded during the
first three days of June. Sporadic ambushes continued
throughout the month, but the upsurge of Volunteer
activities during May and June looked more serious than
it was from Dublin Castle and Westminster. The areas in
which the I.R.A. could operate were becoming strictly
limited. In many parts of the country units dropped out of
the fight and agreed to local truces. Dry summer weather
had hardened the ground and made it possible for
military and police transport to drive round the road blocks
and trenches, and even to travel on the mountain roads
which had hitherto been impassable. The long summer
evenings gave the Flying Columns only a few hours of
respite from harrying attacks. Arms and ammunition were
scarce everywhere and Liam Lynch, and other Southern

44. The Burning of the Custom House 25th May, 1921: This symbolical act emphasised the senseless-ness of the struggle, but did not seem remarkable enough to stop people from cycling home to lunch.

45. King George V had become dissatisfied with the Government's handling of Ireland. On 22nd June, 1921 he came to Belfast to open the Northern Parliament, and make a memorable appeal for peace.

46. *Above:* In the relaxed atmosphere of the day after the Truce, on 11th July, 1921, the dreaded Auxiliaries mingle with the crowds, and carry nothing more lethal than a camera. Scenes like this alarmed I.R.A. leaders who had to consider the possibility of renewed warfare if negotiations failed.

47. *Left:* An Historic Hoisting. The negotiations are over, the Anglo-Irish Treaty has been signed, and on 22nd January, 1922, William T. Cosgrave, first President of the Irish Free State, climbs on to the roof of the City Hall Dublin to fly the City Colours.

48. *Below:* The end of the affair? The Irish Free State Army takes over Dublin Castle. A Free State Officer makes arrangements with a British Officer, while some of the first recruits for the Free State Army wait and look round them with a wild surmise.

Commanders, came to Dublin to report to G.H.Q. that enemy pressure and shortage of ammunition were making it impossible to continue the fight.

Morale began to crack as the number of prisoners mounted. A field service notebook of a Volunteer Commander in mid-Limerick indicates some of the problems that he had to face at that time. General lawlessness and looting by Volunteers were on the increase. There was, for example: 'Martin Nolan living on his wits, cut a goat in two with a bill hook, broke windows, generally drunk, plenty of money to spend, has family and supports them. He asked J. Wayle to get a few to go with him and they would earn plenty of money. People generally afraid of him. Does looting in Mid-Tipp area.' He reports that no recruiting can be done and that there were many desertions. A unit has refused to burn a large house when ordered and roads are not being properly cut. The men do not understand the use of the grenade, and fifty per cent of one company do not know how to handle a rifle. The locals are talking too much, and a Major comes from Cork every week to pay informers.

The leaders doubted whether the I.R.A. could survive another summer campaign even if the threatened reinforcements were not sent from England. But all was not lost. The movement against the Government's policy was growing in England, where Ireland was in the news every day, in one form or another. The Volunteers, for example, again sought to draw attention to their cause by cutting the telegraph and telephone wires between Liverpool and Manchester, and the signal lines at over a dozen places on suburban railway lines near London: General Crozier was making a small income for himself by writing the same article about the Trim looting and the Drumcondra murders so often that many people might have supposed that nothing else had happened in Ireland; the Reverend Conrad Noel, the first of the 'red' Anglican clergymen, flew the Red Flag and the Sinn Fein Flag from his church in Thaxted and provoked some well-publicised disturbances in rural Essex. On a more responsible level, *The Manchester Guardian*, on the 14th June, commented: 'Do not let us imagine that the policy which is favoured by some of the Government advisers of making great military drives, setting up blockhouses and concentration camps would bring us to anything but disaster and disgrace.'

Debates on Ireland in the House became increasingly bitter and frequently lapsed into farce. On the same day, Sir Hamar Greenwood rose to answer a question about the Black and Tans and had begun: 'I am going to stand up again for these men today. . . .' when Mr. Jack Jones, a Labour member, who was a cockney by birth and an Irishman by blood, interposed: 'Three cheers for the chief assassins.' Considerable uproar followed and there were loud cries of 'Withdraw'. The Speaker said that he had occasion before to warn the Honourable Member that he was not entitled to make these interjections, and Mr. Jones replied that he was not willing to withdraw and was willing to go out. As he left the Chamber he turned, and roared at the assembled members: 'Goodnight all you assassins.' A Coalition member shouted back angrily: 'You're a dirty dog', and Mr. Jones, unabashed, replied: 'You're nothing but a damned gang of assassins, the whole lot of you.' An Arab deputation which had come to a visit to the House to study the workings of British democracy was impressed by the liveliness of the proceedings.

The peace party had not been idle in Ireland or in England. 'Andy' Cope had had frequent interviews with Arthur Griffith and Professor Séan MacNeil, another veteran Sinn Fein leader in Mountjoy Gaol, and had even met Collins twice in an attempt to find a settlement. Both sides had been trying for many months to enlist the moral support of the Roman Catholic Church to secure a settlement in favour of themselves; but an Apostolic letter to

Cardinal Logue from Pope Benedict, published on the 23rd May, stated that the policy of the Holy See was: 'To take sides with neither of the contending parties. We exhort the English as well as the Irish to calmly consider whether the time has not arrived to abandon violence and treat of some means of mutual agreement.'

De Valera hoped to secure the support of some of the Dominion Premiers who were assembling in London for an Imperial Conference. General Smuts made a secret visit to Dublin and urged de Valera, disappointingly but not surprisingly, to accept a settlement similar to that which ended the Boer War. Smuts was deeply interested in the Irish situation, although he later described the Sinn Fein leaders as 'small men', and discussed it with the Prime Minister, and with King George V who was known to be acutely distressed by the Government's treatment of his Irish subjects. A few weeks later the King's attitude to his Cabinet about Ireland was summarised in a report in *The Daily Mail* which was immediately and vehemently denied by, it seemed, almost every interested party capable of issuing a denial, as: 'Now, see here, you chaps. You must do something. You cannot shoot all the people in Ireland. We cannot have our people killed like this. You must be on to your jobs and accomplish something.' These were, nevertheless, known to be the private views of the constitutional Monarch.

Cracks appeared on the war party's front in London. Even Sir Henry Wilson, who had warmly greeted the decision to extend martial law to the whole of the country, began to doubt the wisdom of this policy, which had been met with almost unanimous opposition by the British Press. He was also worried by the growing number of regular officers and men who, when posted to Ireland, applied not to be sent there. He told the Secretary of State for War, Sir Laming Worthington-Evans, who had succeeded Winston Churchill in a Cabinet reshuffle in February, that 'unless we had England entirely on our side, I would strongly advise that we should not attempt martial law in all its severity'. He was disturbed by a debate in the House of Lords on the 21st June, on a motion by Lord Donoughmore, an Irish peer, 'that this House is of the opinion that the situation in Ireland urgently requires that His Majesty's Government should determine forthwith what amendments they are prepared to propose, and authorise negotiations to terminate the present deadlock'. In spite of a powerful speech defending the Government by the Lord Chancellor, Lord Birkenhead, the motion had only been defeated by the narrow majority of sixty-six to fifty-seven. Sir Henry interpreted this as 'another sign that the country was not whole-heartedly in favour of flattening out the rebels'. The Secretary of State told him that England was not on their side and could not be got on to it, and Sir Henry concluded 'that it would be madness to try to flatten out the rebels'.

It was as well for the peace party that he and General Macready failed to realise that the Irish Republican Army was already at its last gasp. Their insistence that only a massive all-out action, involving great loss of life and expense, could put the Volunteers out of action was, paradoxically, the decisive argument for the settlement that neither of them wanted. Richard Mulcahy, the I.R.A.'s Chief of Staff, did not share their illusions and said in the debates on the Treaty in the Dáil in 1922: 'We have suffered a defeat.'

The deadlock which had so long prevented the opening of negotiations was finally broken by the King. On the 22nd June, the day on which Sir Henry Wilson abandoned hopes of coercion, King George V went to Belfast to open the first Parliament of Northern Ireland, where he turned an occasion, which might have inflamed feelings, into a source of hope. He had declined to read the draft speech prepared for him in Dublin Castle, because it seemed to him to lack humanity, and he wished the words he used to appeal to

all his Irish subjects, not merely to those in the North.
General Smuts had been privately summoned to Bucking-
ham Palace to prepare a new draft. No one doubted the
King's sincerity when he said with obvious emotion in
Belfast:

> I speak from a full heart when I pray that my coming
> to Ireland today may prove to be the first steps towards
> an end of strife amongst her people, whatever their
> race or creed. In that hope I appeal to all Irishmen to
> pause, to stretch out the hand of forbearance and con-
> ciliation, to forgive and to forget, and to join in making
> for the land which they love a new era of peace, content-
> ment, and good-will. It is my earnest desire that in
> Southern Ireland too there may ere long take place a
> parallel to what is now passing in this hall; that there a
> similar occasion may present itself and a similar ceremony
> be performed.
>
> For this the Parliament of the United Kingdom has in
> the fullest measure provided the powers; for this the
> Parliament of Ulster is pointing the way. The future lies
> in the hands of my Irish people themselves. May this
> historic gathering be the prelude of a day in which the
> Irish people, North and South, under one Parliament or
> two, as those Parliaments may themselves decide, shall
> work together in common love for Ireland upon the sure
> foundation of mutual justice and respect.

Nothing in the King's speech persuaded Sinn Fein to
abandon its principles, but another event in Dublin on the
evening of the same day brought negotiations nearer. A
raiding party of the Worcestershire Regiment picked up a
suspicious individual in Blackrock, near Dublin. He was
later identified as de Valera. Dublin Castle had been given
strict instructions to prevent his arrest, and for many weeks
had feared that he would elude their surveillance and get
caught or, worse still, be shot. He was released on the

following day, by order of the Castle; but the news that he had been arrested and released seemed to people, who did not know of the secret arrangement, a sure sign of an immediate settlement. Troops and police, who had been led to believe that de Valera was the chief assassin in the 'murder gang', were astonished at his release, and they wondered why they were in Ireland.

In Dublin Castle Sir John Anderson and 'Andy' Cope pressed for a conference without restrictions, and in England the peace front extended from the King in Buckingham Palace to the Labour Party in conference at Brighton, where it called for the withdrawal of British troops from Ireland and the election of an Irish Constituent Assembly, and in the Press, from *The Times* to *The Daily Herald*. The leader of the Conservative Party, Sir Austen Chamberlain, and Birkenhead, the Lord Chancellor who, in the House of Lords, only twenty-four hours earlier had promised to fight to the bitter end, both urged Lloyd George that to intensify or continue coercion was not compatible with the spirit of the King's speech. On the 24th June, Lord Stamfordham, the King's Private Secretary, went to see Lloyd George and to impress upon him: 'Now is the time to endeavour to bring about a reconciliation. Unless something is done, the effect of the King's speech will die away. There is not a moment to be lost.' In the evening of the same day Lloyd George wrote to de Valera:

> . . . to convey the following invitation to you, as the chosen leader of the great majority in Southern Ireland, and to Sir James Craig, the Premier of Northern Ireland:

> (1) That you should attend a conference here in London, in company with Sir James Craig, to explore to the utmost the possibility of a settlement.
> (2) That you should bring with you for the purpose ny colleagues whom you select. The Government will,

[214]

of course, give a safe conduct to all who may be chosen to participate in the conference.

We make this invitation with a fervent desire to end the ruinous conflict which has for centuries divided Ireland, and embittered the relations of the peoples of these two islands, who ought to live in neighbourly harmony with each other, and whose co-operation would mean so much, not only to the Empire, but to humanity.

Meanwhile ambush and arson were pursuing their routine course. On the 24th June the I.R.A. mined and derailed a train in which part of the King's escort was returning to the South after the opening of the Northern Parliament. Four troopers of the 10th Royal Hussars were killed, twenty wounded, and eighty horses either killed or so badly injured that they had to be destroyed in one of the I.R.A.'s more notable victories. Peace was still in the balance. On the 28th June the Southern Parliament formally met in accordance with the terms of the Government of Ireland Act. The only members to answer the summons were fifteen senators nominated by the Viceroy and four members for Trinity College, Dublin. The proceedings lasted only a few minutes, and this short-lived Parliament adjourned, never to meet again. On the same day de Valera replied to Lloyd George in a letter which gave heart to the war party at Westminster and to the War Office, who were down but not out:

> ... I am in consultation with such of the principal representatives of our nation as are available. We most earnestly desire to help in bringing about a lasting peace between the peoples of these two islands, but see no avenue by which it can be reached if you deny Ireland's essential unity, and set aside the principle of national self-determination.

De Valera summoned a number of Loyalist leaders, including Lord Middleton and Sir James Craig, Prime

Minister of the Northern Irish Government, to a conference in the Dublin Mansion House. Sir James Craig declined. The Orangemen were suspicious of these manœuvres, and John Andrews, the Ulster Minister for Home Affairs, said bluntly: 'If de Valera and his people want to give the people peace, it is up to them not us. In the interests of peace we have taken a Parliament we never wanted. . . . If they want peace, why don't they do the same?'

The Conference met on the 4th July. The Stars and Stripes flag was flown from the Mansion House on de Valera's orders 'in appreciation of the sympathy and aid given to our people by their friends in the United States'. Americans had contributed three million dollars to the Dáil Loan, and had subscribed £1 million to a relief organisation called 'The White Cross' which had been established in Dublin at the beginning of the year. Irish-American propagandists had also been vocal and powerful enough to bring pressure to bear on their Government, and keep the issue of Ireland alive in Anglo-American diplomatic exchanges. Most of the imprisoned Republican leaders had been released and were able to attend. Ten members of the R.I.C., eleven of the I.R.A. and seven 'spies and informers' had been killed in the four days since de Valera had summoned it. Three Loyalists' houses had also been burned, and over £200,000 damage caused in fires started by Volunteers in Argyle Street, Glasgow. But the people of Ireland were in a state of jubilant expectancy, and Dubliners demonstrated enthusiastically outside the Mansion House to the despair of the I.R.A. leaders, who realised how difficult it would be to restart the fight if the negotiations failed. On the 5th July General Smuts returned to Dublin *incognito* in the character of 'Mr. Smith', at de Valera's request. He found that de Valera distrusted Lloyd George's offer, and was disposed to refuse it. He warned him that if he did, he would turn public opinion against himself all over the world, and even in Ireland. He argued strongly against the Irish demand for an independent Republic, and made it plain that he thought that what was good enough for South Africa was good enough for Ireland. De Valera, according to General Smuts, said: 'If the status of a Dominion is offered me, I will use all our machinery to get the Irish people to accept it.' Either General Smuts misheard him or de Valera changed his mind, for a year later he used all his machinery to get the Irish people to refuse Dominion status, which had been granted by the Anglo-Irish Treaty, and launched the country into a bitter civil war.

General Smuts returned to London and, in a report to Lloyd George, strongly advised an immediate truce, as he felt that only the cessation of hostilities could abate the bitter feelings that had been aroused.

The Conference adjourned on the 5th July, and Lord Middleton went to London to see Lloyd George. For two days it seemed that peace might founder on the snag which had wrecked the earlier negotiations—the demand that the I.R.A. should surrender its arms; but Lloyd George, who had refused to consider an armed truce, suddenly capitulated. The Conference resumed its deliberations on the 8th July. In the late afternoon General Macready drove in an open car to the Mansion House and forced his way through a throng of cheering Dubliners. An old woman even seized his hand and kissed it. He was not impressed by this ovation. 'It was a hot day,' he wrote, 'the crowd was fairly tightly packed together and the resulting atmosphere was not pleasant.' The terms of the Truce were decided at General Macready's headquarters on the following day, and were to take effect at midday on the 11th July. De Valera announced in a telegram to Lloyd George on the 10th that he would be in London for a conference on the 12th. The 'Tan' war was over.

Eleventh-hour warriors of the I.R.A. hurried to get their last shots in. On the 9th they killed the daughter of a retired R.I.C. sergeant in a raid on his house in Tipperary, burned a Loyalist house in Wexford, and wounded one soldier and one member of the R.I.C. On the 10th they wounded one soldier, one member of the R.I.C. and took an Irish ex-officer out of his house and shot him. In a last wild flurry of activity on the 11th, between first light and midday, Volunteers killed five British soldiers and wounded one in Cork, killed three and wounded one in Kerry, and shot two 'convicted spies', and wounded two soldiers and three members of the R.I.C. in scattered attacks elsewhere. Pieras Beaslai, then the I.R.A.'s Director of Publicity, has written: 'These belated exhibitions of prowess, with no military objectives, when the danger seemed past, reflected no credit on Irishmen, but they were only the beginning of a period which patriotic Irishmen feel little pride in recording.'

But these exploits were no different in kind from hundreds of others in the preceding eighteen months, and while many Volunteers fought the good fight for their country's freedom, many more had, unhappily, relapsed into a moral anarchy unconnected with any political or social or practical end other than the muzzle of a gun. 'Dublin Castle Surrenders,' the Irish Press announced exultantly, and the young men who thought they had achieved this victory all by themselves with their Mausers, Mannlinchers, pistols and rook rifles, kept their weapons for another day. 'So long,' a Black and Tan shouted to the people on the quay as he left Ireland. 'I'll soon be back to separate you.' But it was not necessary. If there had been any doubt of it before, the Irish were soon to prove in their Civil War that anything the Black and Tans could do, they could do better. By the time they had finished they had quite extinguished the revolutionary flames lit by the Proclamation of Easter, 1916. Ireland made the first, and the least effective, of the post-war revolutions. The country, apparently exhausted by the effort of striking off the shackles of oppression, relapsed gradually into the lethargy and hopelessness for which the men from over the sea had always been blamed.

Anglo-Irish relations from 1916 to 1921 make a melancholy story of which the moral seems to be that politicians tend to follow precedent like lawyers: they do not learn from experience, but make the same mistakes over and over again. Kitchener could have ended the Boer War in March, 1901, if the Government of the day had taken his advice; but the war dragged on for another fifteen months before peace was concluded on the terms he had urged. Eighteen years later Lloyd George pursued a policy in Ireland that he had vigorously condemned when it was applied to South Africa. He had 'murder by the throat' and would not listen to men who advocated terms on which the Treaty was finally based. The rules of this political game have varied little from the outbreak of the Boer War in 1899 to the Suez crisis of 1956.

The British Government could not put a foot right in Ireland. The executions and arrests after the 1916 Rebellion aroused Irish nationalist feeling. The threat of conscription in 1917 united all Irishmen, outside Ulster, from the Hierarchy to the marxists in the Irish Labour Party, against the Government, and drove the majority of the men of military age into Sinn Fein. The arrest of the Sinn Fein leaders in 1918, including de Valera who was never a full Republican, and Arthur Griffith, who was a monarchist, left the conduct of affairs to the extremists of the Irish Republican Brotherhood and, in particular, to Michael Collins. The result of this repression was the Sinn Fein electoral victory of December, 1918. A general amnesty, at this point, and the offer of terms very much less generous than those agreed by the Anglo-Irish Treaty three years later might well have succeeded where the military, the Black and Tans and the Auxiliaries failed, and have kept Ireland inside the Union; but, instead, the extremists in Ireland declared an independent Irish Republic, and in

England Lloyd George introduced the Better Government of Ireland Bill, for which no Irishman voted.

The course of events thereafter was largely dictated by Michael Collins. He, more than any man, was responsible for the hostilities which the Irish people did not want, and which fortified the opponents of Irish self-government in Ulster and Westminster. Later, when he defended the Treaty in 1922, he wrote: 'To me it would have been a criminal act to refuse to allow the Irish nation to give its opinion as to whether it would accept this settlement or resume hostilities'; but in 1918 he did not consider it a criminal act to deny the Irish nation the right to decide whether it wanted the hostilities started at all. It is useless to speculate how much Ireland might have saved and gained by a disciplined campaign of civil resistance. She would have had powerful allies in England, where pro-Irish sentiment was strong, and could have been effective even without the stimulation of the Black and Tans.

Lloyd George's Irish policy, or the lack of it, presented him with a campaign of violence which had to be suppressed, and the demand for a Republic which left him no room for negotiation. Had Ireland been the only problem in a troubled world, he might have found his way through this impasse sooner. He might have freed himself at any time from his barren 'murder gang' mentality, for which Michael Collins provided considerable support, and brought peace with the offer of a generous measure of self-government; but in the press of domestic and international affairs, he did not address himself seriously to the problem of Ireland until the spring of 1921. The Black and Tans were his makeshift solution. They were, with all their faults, far easier to bear than would have been the 'free hand' which Sir Henry Wilson and the soldiers demanded, and which Lloyd George refused to grant; and they wore the I.R.A. down until it was prepared to negotiate.

In this process of attrition, between January, 1920, and

the Truce on the 11th July, 1921, the Irish casualties have been estimated at about 700 killed and over 800 wounded. A count of named casualties, as they were reported day by day in the Press at the time, is necessarily incomplete, but it suggests that about half the total were Volunteers and half civilians. It adds up to 276 Volunteers killed, and 288 civilians either shot dead in affrays, found dead labelled as spies, or taken out and murdered by masked men on one side or the other. The British casualties in the same period were 366 police and 162 soldiers killed and 600 police and 566 soldiers wounded. Recruiting for the Royal Irish Constabulary stopped on the 11th July, and the withdrawals of the Black and Tans and Auxiliaries began in October. Twenty more police were killed and forty wounded by trigger-happy Volunteers before the Royal Irish Constabulary was finally disbanded in January, 1922. By that time bitter and tortuous negotiations had ended in the signing of the Anglo-Irish Treaty on the 6th December, 1921. The Treaty was the first of a long and complicated series of moves which broke the six-hundred-year-old British connection. De Valera rejected the Treaty and plunged the country into civil war, because he favoured a form of oath of allegiance which was almost indistinguishable, except to metaphysicians, from the oath required by the Treaty. Never were lives spent to less purpose, and by taking up arms for his minority view, de Valera gave a precedent to the young men who have taken up arms against his own Government. The oath of allegiance was abolished in 1933; the new Constitution of 1937 established Ireland 'a sovereign, independent and democratic state' in external association with the British Commonwealth; in 1938 Great Britain surrendered the three naval bases in Southern Ireland which had been secured by the Treaty; and the Dáil's Republic of Ireland Act of 1949 finally severed the Irish Free State from the British Commonwealth, but not the Irish from Great Britain.

[221]

The Treaty was, thus, both an end and a beginning. The major credit for such settlement as it provided was accorded to Lloyd George, but some at least should attach to the Black and Tans. They had played a decisive part in the long, sad history of Anglo-Irish relations. They had, indeed, made Ireland 'a hell for rebels to live in', and had carried out the Government's policy so successfully that the Prime Minister was forced to abandon it and come to the conference table. The I.R.A. never beat the 'Tans', an old Volunteer commander has said. 'It was the British people who did it.'

The men who achieved this remarkable military and political result returned home to join the growing army of the unemployed. Some of them later enlisted in the Palestine Police, and one became its commanding officer. At least two ended their lives at the end of the hangman's rope, and another ex-Black and Tan murderer committed suicide before the police could arrest him. Most of them were no better and no worse than the rest of us. Black and Tans are made, not born. Nearly all of them enjoyed the spectacle of Irishmen cutting one another's throats in the Civil War of 1922-23 with sardonic satisfaction, and without being aware that they had helped to brutalise the young men of Ireland and were at least partly responsible for it. None of them could know that he had been an actor in the first scenes of a post-war drama that was to continue in Egypt, India, Burma, Indonesia, Indo-China, Malaya, Kenya, the Gold Coast, Cyprus and Algeria and is still far from finished.

BIBLIOGRAPHY

Barry, Tom, *Guerilla Days in Ireland*, Irish Press (*1944*).

Beaslai, Pieras, *Michael Collins and the making of a new Ireland*, Phoenix, Dublin (*1926*).

Blackwoods, *Tales of the R.I.C.* (*1922*).

Breen, Dan, *My Fight for Irish Freedom*, Talbot Press, Dublin (*1929*)

Bretherton, C. H. E. *The Real Ireland*, Black, (*1925*).

Bromage, Mary, *De Valera and the March of a Nation*, Hutchinson (*1956*)

Callwell, C. E., *Field Marshall Sir Henry Wilson. His Life and Diaries*, Cassell (*1927*).

Clarkson, J. Dunsmore, *Labour and Nationalism in Ireland*, Columbia University, New York (*1925*).

Crozier, Brigadier-General F. P., *Ireland for Ever*, Cape (*1932*).

Ewart, Wilfrid, *A Journey in Ireland*, Putnams (*1922*).

Figgis, Darrell, *Recollections of the Irish War*, Benn (*1927*).

Hammond, J. L., *The Terror in Action*, Nation and Athenaeum (*1921*).

Hogan, David., *The Four Glorious Years*, Irish Press, Dublin (*1953*).

I. O. (C. J. C. Street), *The Administration of Ireland 1921*, Philip Allan (*1921*).

Macready, General, the Rt. Hon. Sir Nevil, *Annals of an active life*, Hutchinson (*1924*).

Martin, Hugh, *Ireland in Insurrection*, Daniel O'Connor (*1921*).

Nicolson, Harold, *King George the Fifth. His Life and Reign*, Constable (*1952*).

O'Connor, Batt, *With Michael Collins in the Fight for Irish Independence*, Peter Davies (*1929*).

O'Connor, Frank, *The Big Fellow*, Nelson (*1937*).

O'Connor, Rt. Hon. Sir James, *History of Ireland 1798–1924*, Arnold (*1925*).

O'Donoghue, Florence, *The Story of Liam Lynch and the Republican Army 1916–23*, Irish Press (*1954*).

O'Faoláin, Sean, *Constance Markievicz*, Cape (*1934*).

O'Hegarty, P. S., *The Victory of Sinn Fein*, Talbot Press, Dublin (*1924*).

O'Malley, Ernie, *On Another Man's Wound*, Rich & Cowan (*1938*).

Pakenham, Frank, *Peace by Ordeal*, Cape (*1935*).

Phillips, W. Allison, *The Revolution in Ireland 1906–23*, Longmans (*1923*).

BIBLIOGRAPHY

Riddell, Lord, *Intimate Diary of the Peace Conference and After*, Gollancz (*1933*).

Robinson, Sir Henry Augustus, *Memories Wise and Otherwise*, Cassell (*1923*).

Street, C. J. C., *Ireland in 1922*, Philip Allan (*1922*).

Talbot, Hayden, *Michael Collins' Own Story*, Hutchinson (*1923*).

Taylor, Rex, *Michael Collins. An Introduction.* Hutchinson (*1958*).

Usher, Arland, *The Face and Mind of Ireland*, Gollancz (*1949*).

Winter, Sir Ormonde, *Winter's Tale*, Richards Press (*1955*).

Index

INDEX

INDEX

[227]

INDEX